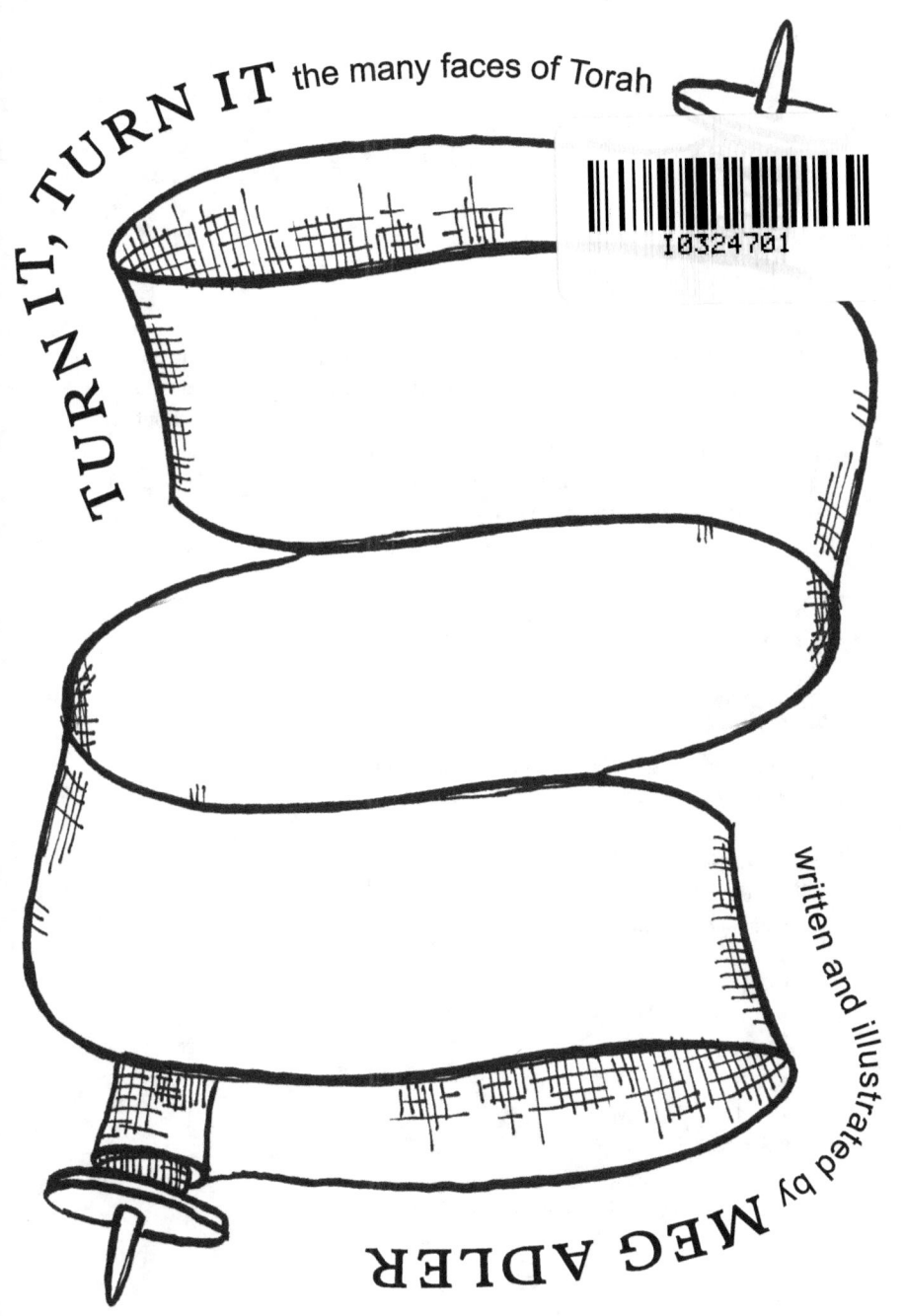

TURN IT, TURN IT
the many faces of Torah

written and illustrated by MEG ADLER

SECOND EDITION

Turn It, Turn It — SECOND EDITION
by Meg Adler

adler.meg@gmail.com
(510) 418-0354

turnitturnit.substack.com

Copyright © 2024 by Meg Adler

All rights reserved. No part of this book may be reproduced, stored in an electronic retrieval system, or transcribed in any form or by any means, electronic or mechanical, including photocopying and recording, without prior written permission of the publisher, except for the inclusion of quotations in a review. If you have purchased an electronic copy, please print only for the personal use of the purchaser.

Published by

ALTERNADOX PRESS

All inquiries about this and other Alternadox publications should be addressed to:

Rabbi Gavriel Goldfeder
Alternadox Publishers
heyrabbi@gmail.com

alternadox.net

ISBN 978-0-9839051-6-5

Designed by Lily Kravetz
lilykravetz.com

Printed in the United States of America

FOR MY TEACHERS

TABLE OF CONTENTS

FIRST WORDS

Acknowledgements 1
Introduction 3

GROUNDING

What Is Torah? 10
When Do We Read Torah? 19
Let's Talk About "God" 24

TORAH IS A THING

Ode to a Sefer Torah 34
The Tree of Life 38
Faces 42
Honey Under Your Tongue 44
Fire on Fire 48
Melody and Meaning 52

TORAH IS A TIMEKEEPER

Calendar of Stories 58
We Also Read Joshua 62
There Is No Timeline in Torah 65
My Dad's Chumash 68

TORAH IS A RELATIONSHIP

Yes, You Are Your Brother's Keeper 72
Make For Yourself a Teacher 77
Students 81
People of The Book 86
When Torah Feels Like a Bully 90

TORAH IS A DOCUMENT

Ezra's Scroll 97
Like Us, Full of Contradictions 101
A New Argument About Those Lines in Leviticus 109
Take Two 113

TORAH IS A PLAYGROUND

What is This Story Not Telling Me? 120
Modern Midrash: Eve's Launch 124
Modern Midrash: Na'amah's Nightmare 127
Modern Midrash: The Day Miriam Died 131
Modern Midrash: Huldah The In-between 135
Modern Midrash: Jehoshebeath and The Boy King 140
What Does 'Judaism' Say About This? 143
Playground 150
The Belief Game 153

LAST THINGS

Afterword: Write It, Do It 160
Bibliography 164

FIRST WORDS

ACKNOWLEDGEMENTS

To Rabbi Gavriel Goldfeder: thank you for taking a chance on these words. Thank you for your spirit and irreverent reverence.

To my LABA cohort and leaders: thank you for inspiring me with your art and interpretations. Thank you for listening. Thank you for all that you have broken.

To my teachers and friends: thank you for challenging me — for asking my opinion and actually telling me yours. Thank you for correcting me and cheering me on. Thank you for tolerating endless self-promotion and article links and texts with which I'm so determined to ensnare your spirit. In particular, I'd like to thank those who have been swimming in these big Torah waters with me. You know who you are.

To Mom and Julia: thank you for letting me share my triumphs and tumbles. Thank you for reading everything I send and always being the first to sign up for my latest thing. I love you.

To Rachel: what would Rachel say, I ask myself? What text would she choose? What question would she ask? What joke would she crack? I know for sure, no matter where you are now, you are teaching Torah. You are poking fun at that new student who gets it. I miss you with every word I write.

To Colleen: thank you for being my b'shert. Thank you for sitting next to me as I write and we watch rom coms and bad reality tv. Thank you for making sure we never blow out the Shabbat candles.

INTRODUCTION

If your Torah had not been my delight, I would have perished in my suffering. — Psalm 119:92

This book will not teach you everything you need to know about Torah. It is not pretending to be anything other than a conversation. An invitation. An introduction. Allow me to introduce you.

The Torah is a wild document—a wilderness. To understand the Torah is like trying to understand your parents. One day, everything makes sense. The next day, it's complicated and you're seeking help from highly trained professionals. Sometimes it's fun and nurturing and playful. Other times, it's painful. As you grow, it grows with you. As you grow, you read it in new and more complex ways.

To read the Torah is to turn it. To see how the light catches it in each season of the year–each season of your life. It is an orientation towards the world. When you come to the end, you start again at the beginning, no matter how many times you have done so before. To study Torah is *not* to say, *I know, I know*. To study Torah is to say, *Tell me more.*

Ben Bag Bag said: Turn it over, and [again] turn it over, for all is therein. And look into it; And become gray and old therein; And do not move away from it, for you have no better portion than it.[1]

To turn something over — once, twice, fifty-seven times — to explore it requires curiosity and perseverance. I am reminded of all of those times as a child when I lost a shoe or book or Barbie.* I'd look and look but never find whatever it was. My mother would invariably ask if I looked behind and under things. Nope. I mostly just hoped what I'd lost was just sitting in the middle of a room somewhere with a big neon sign over it flashing, Here I am! But of course, it never was. So too with Torah. So too with so many things.

Turn it, turn it means stay curious and keep going. Already, this book you are holding is so clearly about the Torah and so much more than the Torah. I hope you'll see that too.

Derived from its content, form, and practice, the lessons that the Torah teaches are lessons about living a good life. Lessons about how to cultivate our minds and hearts with a balance of humility and audacity. And we were created to learn these lessons. Rabbi Yochanan ben Zakkai says, *If you have learned much Torah, do not take credit for yourself, because it is for this that you were created.*[2] You were created to have extremely deep meaning in your life.

When Ben Bag Bag says *Turn it, turn it,* of course, he means both the text and yourself. Turn yourself around, turn yourself around — see yourself from all angles and consider how infinite you are. Consider how the next minute is not guaranteed. You get to choose what to do with it. Keep reading? Go outside and scream? Both are possible futures. Turn it, turn it.

One weekend I was teaching my students about the two creation stories in the Book of Genesis (more on that later). I asked how it could be that there are two versions of how the entire universe was created. Many students had brilliant answers, but one in particular stuck with me. *Maybe the two creation stories indicate that we are living in parallel universes and we are only experiencing one version of* life. *Somewhere out there we are living our lives in new ways.* What a thought! I was thrilled. I had never heard that interpretation before. *Indeed, maybe.*

Turn it, turn it, for everything is in it–even another universe. A rebirth of our Jewish textual tradition. A future that welcomes all voices and gives everyone the tools. A new you.

***

Why did I write this book now? I wrote this book because it is not a casual thing to be Jewish. It is complicated and full of compromise. It is also full of purpose. The purpose contained within being Jewish is multifaceted, and it is integral to who we are.

In an Instagram post on June 24, 2022, Rabbi Shais Rishon, also known as MaNishtana, wrote that *Judaism is primarily a religion of responsibilities.* I agree. Among many other things, to be Jewish means to be responsible for stewarding the earth and honoring the sacredness of every living being. We are responsible for caring for our families. We are responsible for seeking justice and pursuing it. We are responsible to ourselves–to keep learning, to remember and teach that we are dust and ashes and yet the whole world was created for us.[3] To be Jewish means to say 100 blessings a day and keep the Sabbath — to take one day a week to rest, reflect, sing, pray, and revel in life. To be Jewish is to stare down the oppression and pain your own tradition causes and has caused and ask yourself, how do we move ourselves in a direction of healing and true wholeness? What are we willing to leave behind to pursue a more just Jewish life for tomorrow?

Several years ago I read a short quote by Dr. Bill Damon, the Director of Stanford's Center on Adolescence, that has stuck with me. Damon says, *The biggest problem growing up today is not actually stress; it's meaninglessness.*[4]

I fear he is right. Stress isn't necessarily bad. But when we feel we are headed towards the fire-filled-furnace-of-a-world we keep hearing about in every tweet and breaking news segment? That is something else. This crash course toward meaninglessness manifests in so many ways: we are living in a time when growing old means becoming increasingly inconvenient instead of wise. The questions commonly asked are not about how we can honor our elders and learn from their experiences, but what should we do with them—where should we put them? We are living in a time where college applications are an expensive crap-shoot and college itself turns out to be not much better for so many. Kids watch politicians name-call on social media instead of showing true examples of leadership and moral courage. There is a sense of chaos–that nothing is sacred. That we should all go home now, snuggle up, get high, and wait for the end times. I fervently disagree.

After sharing Dr. Damon's quote with some of my teenage students, I was saddened to hear first-hand that while some disagreed that meaninglessness was the *biggest* problem, all corroborated that they are all too familiar with that feeling. For a person of any age, a lack of purpose can creep in and rob us of strength, creative potential, joy, and, worst of all, life. But this is especially disturbing when people who are so young become so jaded.

This book is my attempt to share meaning with you by reintroducing you to the bedrock of Jewish life. I want a chance for you and I to make meaning as Jews have done for thousands of years through storytelling, study, and discovering that sacred spark that connects us when we engage in words of Torah. Encountering The Divine. This book represents my attempt to reimagine Torah study. Imagining something always starts with that first moment. This book is a first moment.

This book is a manifestation of my hope, too. As the revolutionary exegete Rabbi Steven Greenberg writes, *There is great hope in a tradition that loves good questions even more than good answers.*[5] I'm writing this book because I take hope very seriously and frankly, we need more of it in our world. I find hope in Torah study.

Then there is this oft-repeated piece of wisdom:

[Rabbi Tarfon] used to say: *It is not your duty to finish the work, but neither are you at liberty to neglect it.*[6]

In other words, I'm writing this because, right now, I have to.

✴✴✴

So what is in this book? It starts with a section to ground those unfamiliar with Torah. What is Torah? When do we read it? After that, the book quickly opens up into a series of short essays about the many dimensions of Torah. We start with the section called Torah is a Thing and quickly move from a reflection on material culture to the various metaphors used to understand our ancient writings. Then, we consider how the Torah keeps time for the Jewish calendar year and in other transcendently fabulous ways. Next, we consider how we are in relationship to Torah and how Torah can mediate some of the most meaningful human relationships. After that, we look at the Torah through a historical lens and consider how (if not given directly at Mt. Sinai/Horeb) this document came together. Finally, we enter the playground that is Torah study and creative interpretation.

However, the categories that organize this book are semipermeable membranes and there is no doubt that many essays might belong under multiple headings. Such is Torah! It's all happening. My hope is these categories will serve as new perspectives — new *faces* of the Torah, to use an image from our tradition.

A final disclaimer: there is no way to include everything about Torah in this slim volume. I hope you are left hungry. This book is intended to be the hors d'oeuvre, appetizer, forshpeis.

So, I leave you here to take a bite. Start anywhere. Take your time. And may you turn it, turn it.

GROUNDING

WHAT IS TORAH?

Torah in sum is all the vastness and variety of the Jewish Tradition... Any effort then at describing the full meaning of Torah for committed Jews is foredoomed to failure. Yet the attempt must be ventured.
— Rabbi Milton Steinberg[7]

Torah is a word that can mean several different things. To start, it comes from the root word yarah meaning to throw, shoot, or cast. In a certain conjugation, it becomes Torah, meaning direction, teaching, instruction. But what is it referring to? In simplest terms, it is referring to four different yet overlapping things.

TORAH: THE FIVE BOOKS OF MOSES

Torah refers to the Five Books of Moses, AKA the Pentateuch:

* Genesis/Bereishit
* Exodus/Shemot
* Leviticus/Vayikra
* Numbers/Bamidbar
* Deuteronomy/D'varim

These five books cover a lot of ground, from the creation of the world to the death of Moses (spoiler alert). This is what is written on a sefer Torah (Torah scroll) or in a chumash (a bound book copy). This is generally what we mean when we say the Torah.

You will find and enjoy an *extremely* redacted summary of each of the Five Books of Moses at the end of this chapter.

TORAH: THE HEBREW BIBLE

Torah refers to the entire Hebrew Bible, AKA TaNaKh AKA Written Torah AKA Old Testament AKA Hebrew Scriptures (and more, as we'll see).[8] In the Jewish world, we use the acronym TaNaKh which stands for Torah (the Five Books of Moses just mentioned), Nevi'im (Prophets) and Ketuvim (Writings). My teacher, Rachel Brodie z"l, described TaNaKh as an anthology.

We tend to think of the Bible as a single volume but it is actually an anthology covering the greatest hits of Hebrew literary production spanning nine centuries. It includes historiography, narrative fiction, law, prophecy in prose and poetry, aphorisms, laments, battle hymns, love songs, genealogical tables, etiological tales, and more. [9]

As Brodie says, TaNaKh is more like a collection or playlist than a single piece of text. Roughly speaking, Nevi'im and Ketuvim cover the time of the conquest of the Promised Land (that would be the Book of Joshua) to the establishment of the diaspora and rebuilding of the second Temple. In between we get *lots* of drama — more than enough for an HBO™ series. We read about setting up the monarchy with King Saul, King David, and King Solomon. The building of the first Temple in Jerusalem. The split of the kingdom into Israel and Judah. Prophets yelling about how corrupt everyone is. The destruction of the northern kingdom of Israel by the Assyrian Empire and the subsequent lost tribes of Israel. More upset prophets. The destruction of the Temple in Jerusalem by the Babylonians and the exile of the Judeans. Prophets still prophet-ing. Rebuilding the Temple by the few who chose to return. Ezra reading the Torah. The story of Purim in the Book of Esther. And that's just a haphazard synopsis. Here are the books inside of Nevi'im and Ketuvim:

Prophets/Nevi'im

- Joshua
- Judges/Shoftim
- 1 Samuel
- 2 Samuel
- 1 Kings
- 2 Kings
- Isaiah
- Jeremiah
- Ezekiel
- Hosea
- Joel
- Amos
- Obadiah
- Jonah
- Micah
- Nahum
- Habakkuk
- Zephaniah
- Haggai
- Zechariah
- Malachi

Writings/Ketuvim

- Psalms/Tehillim
- Proverbs/Mishlei
- Job
- The Song of Songs/Shir HaShirim
- Ruth
- Lamentations/Eicha
- Ecclesiastes/Kohelet
- Esther
- Daniel
- Ezra
- Nehemiah
- 1 Chronicles
- 2 Chronicles

TORAH: THE ORAL TORAH

Torah refers to everything we have just mentioned (the Written Torah) plus the Oral Torah, which we also call Talmud (the Mishnah and Gemara) and the Midrashim. So, in total, it includes what the early Rabbis wrote down based on their oral traditions, and then what the later rabbis commented upon for hundreds of years. Scholar Jacob Neusner writes

The Hebrew word Mishnah comes from the root shanah, to repeat: the word for the ordinal, second, sheni, has the same root. As the title of the law code of Judah, the Patriarch of Jewish Palestine in the beginning of the third century AD it means "that which is to be learned by repetition," therefore by memory. The further implication is that the Mishnah contains materials which had been memorized and not written down for a very long time. For the Talmudic Sages claimed that to Moses had been revealed two Torahs, or revelations, at Mount Sinai. One was contained in the Scriptures — that is, in written books — and the other in oral traditions learned by repetition and handed on in that manner for many centuries. So the Mishnah was represented by the authority behind it as the second essential part of the whole Torah of Moses.* [10]

Neusner goes on to explain Talmud, the next iteration of Oral Torah, as *a compilation of law and lore created by Palestinian and Babylonian rabbis between the late first and seventh centuries* AD.[11] We could spend an entire book explaining what the Talmud is (Neusner does in his book — go read it!). For the scope of *this* book, such a simple introduction will have to suffice. More on midrash, later.

TORAH: ALL JEWISH WISDOM

Torah refers to all Jewish scholarship and storytelling that ever was and ever will be. In this sense, the book you are holding is Torah. The drashot (sermons) Jewish leaders across the world will give this Shabbat are Torah. The Rugrats™ Passover special that aired during the 90s on Nickelodeon™ was and forever will be Torah.

***

Oy, I already messed up. There is actually a fifth way we refer to the word Torah: Torah as a process — how we study and learn. Torah as a pedagogy. Torah as a practice. This sentiment will be made clear as you continue reading.

Throughout this book, I refer to Torah in different ways. Sometimes I'm specifically talking about the Five Books of Moses and other times I'm talking more generally about Jewish wisdom. Try not to worry too much about which one I'm referring to. The worldbuilding we do inside of Torah relies upon multiple meanings of a single thing. It's only right that the word itself can't sit still.

* * *

SUMMARY OF THE BOOK OF GENESIS/BEREISHIT

Bereishit means In the beginning or With beginning and for sure this book is about beginnings. We start with two accounts of the creation of the world, plants, animals, and people. Adam and Eve are in the Garden of Eden. The serpent. Cain kills Abel. Then we get the stories of Noah's ark and the flood, the tower of Babel, and the beginning of the Hebrews, Abram and Sarai. God tells Abram to leave his home and go to a place God will show them. Abram agrees to a covenant with God, and Abram and Sarai become Abraham and Sarah. Even though they are approximately 100 years old they haven't had a kid yet (except for Ishmael through Sarah's maidservant, Hagar). Abraham and Sarah finally have a son named Isaac who marries Rebekah. Isaac and Rebekah have twins, Jacob (who eventually wrestles with a man and is given the name Israel) and Esau (who is hairy). After much trickery and cunning, Jacob receives the blessing and birthright from his father, marries Leah and Rachel, and together with the help of two more maidservants (Bilhah and Zilpah), they begin a family of 13 children (12 boys and 1 girl, Dinah). The brothers sell Joseph into slavery down in Egypt, but he soon becomes an advisor to Pharaoh (the king of Egypt). There is a famine and all of Joseph's brothers and family move down to Egypt to survive. And thus, we leave the book of Genesis with the Israelites in Egypt.

SUMMARY OF THE BOOK OF EXODUS/SHEMOT

Shemot means Names and this book starts with the names of the 12 children of Jacob/Israel who came down to Egypt. Generations have passed and the Israelites are enslaved in Egypt. Pharaoh declares that all newborn Israelite boys will be thrown in the Nile. Two Egyptian midwives (Shifra and Pu'ah) don't obey Pharaoh and one Israelite mother (Yocheved) has a newborn boy and saves him by putting him in a reed basket in the Nile. Pharaoh's daughter (Batya) rescues him and adopts him and he grows up in the Egyptian court. This boy, of course, is Moses.

One day, after seeing an Egyptian guard beat a Hebrew, Moses snaps and kills the Egyptian. He now has to flee Egypt and ends up becoming a shepherd and starting a family in Midian. Years later, Moses comes across a burning bush through which God tells him to go back to Egypt and free the Israelites. Moses basically gives one million excuses why he isn't the right guy for the job. God counters all the excuses. Moses loses the argument and ends up sending ten terrible plagues upon Egypt until Pharaoh finally lets the Israelites go (cue: the story of Passover). The Israelites escape, come to the Sea of Reeds, God parts the sea, and Moses and Miriam lead them in singing their freedom.

But freedom is also a big, empty, hot desert. The Israelites complain they are thirsty and hungry. They come to a big mountain, Mt. Sinai/Horeb, and God calls Moses up to the top of the mountain. There he receives the Ten Commandments and many other laws (a whopping total of 613). It is here that all of the Israelites enter a covenant with God — they will obey the laws and God will make the Israelites a

holy and prosperous nation. Meanwhile, the people (who are missing Moses, who has been on the mountain for 40 days) start worshiping a golden calf and in a fit of rage, Moses smashes the tablets of the commandments. He makes another set and teaches the Israelites about how to build the big traveling holy tent called the Mishkan AKA the Tabernacle.

SUMMARY OF THE BOOK OF LEVITICUS/VAYIKRA

Vayikra means And [God] called and this book is all about Moses explaining more and more laws and rituals. They just keep coming. We learn about what to do if you break a law or need to ask forgiveness (FYI, the biblical response is generally to sacrifice animals). Of primary importance, we learn about the priests and how they are to work in the Tabernacle. Aaron is ordained as the first priest. What should priests wear? How and when do they offer sacrifices? This is all covered in the priestly onboarding section of this book. You can think of it like an employee handbook for working at the Mishkan.

We learn about the new year (Rosh Hashanah), the day of atonement (Yom Kippur), and three harvest festivals (Sukkot, Passover, and Shavuot). Laws for the shmita (sabbatical year) and jubilee years (every 50th year).

Many of the laws in this book are about purity and making sure the people are spiritually clean. Sexual morality laws. Laws about taking care of the stranger or needy among you. Laws about leaving the corners of your field for people who are hungry to come and eat. Laws about skin disease and quarantining outside of camp. Laws about how to serve and uphold justice. Laws. Laws. Laws.

SUMMARY OF THE BOOK OF NUMBERS/BAMIDBAR

Bamidbar means In the wilderness/desert and is more or less

a collection of stories about the Israelites traveling through the wilderness on the way to the land of Israel, with laws loosely related to those stories interspersed throughout. Moses sends 12 spies to scout out the Promised Land and all but two (Joshua and Caleb) come back shaking in their sandals, afraid of the people living in the land. God says that for this behavior the Israelites will be destined to wander for 40 years until a new generation comes of age that isn't filled with such weenies.

We learn about the King of Moab (Balak) commissioning a prophet (Balaam) to curse the Israelites. Balaam can't curse them but blesses them instead and also his donkey talks along the way. Oh, and before that, this rebel named Korach questions Moses as the singular leader. For his effort, Korach is swallowed up by the earth. Aaron and Miriam also question Moses but only Miriam gets punished by God with leprosy. Aaron gets off with a warning.

Both Aaron and Miriam die. And even though Moses has been putting up with these stiffnecked Israelites and walking up and down mountains and serving as head judge and on and on and on, one day he hits a rock against God's instructions and for that is denied entry into the Promised Land.

SUMMARY OF THE BOOK OF DEUTERONOMY/D'VARIM

D'varim means Words and this book is nothing if not a lot of words, from Moses especially. Let's just say the guy went from *I'm slow of speech* to *And another thing!* Moses recounts pretty much all of the laws to the Israelites and tells them to *Choose life,* meaning, choose to obey God's commandments. Even though Deuteronomy repeats a lot of the laws we get earlier in Torah, there are definitely some changes here and there. You can think of Deuteronomy (which means Second law) as the first time the earlier books of Torah are interpreted. New reasons are given for Shabbat, for example. We get the prayers

Shema and V'ahavta. And at the end of his very long speech, Moses recites a poem and tells the people to write it down and remember it forever. Moses then ascends Mt. Nebo, passes on his leadership role to Joshua, and though *his eyes were undimmed and his vigor unabated*,[12] overlooking the Promised Land, he dies.

To be continued…

WHEN DO WE READ TORAH?

Reading Torah out loud has been a communal event since the time of Ezra, around 444 BCE. Actually, the Book of Deuteronomy is thought to have been read aloud even earlier, around the 600s BCE![13] Of course anyone can pick up the text whenever they please, but prescribed readings bind the Jews to the words and to one another in foundational ways. It's not just about getting through The Book. It's about sharing the experience of reading and listening, together. Torah facilitates community. The following is a basic (and not exhaustive) overview of when we read Torah.

SHABBAT

Most notably we read Torah every Shabbat morning (Saturday morning). We read whatever parasha (portion) is assigned for that day, and we know what is assigned because we are reading in order, from the beginning of the Torah (starting with Simchat Torah in the fall) to the end (ending with Simchat Torah).

Things to know:

* The parasha assigned for that week is called parashat hashavuah.
* The parasha is named after the first significant word or short phrase of the reading.

Every Shabbat we also read a section from the books of the Nevi'im (Prophets) that we call the haftarah reading. Here to explain more is George Robinson, from his book *Essential Judaism*:

The establishment of the Haftarot, the readings from the Prophets that take place after the reading of the [parasha] for the week in the Torah service, probably took place before the destruction of the Second Temple. Folklore claims that the readings have their roots in the anti-Semitic persecutions of the second century BCE, when the Syrian monarch Antiochus Epiphanes (the one the Maccabees rebelled against) banned the public reading or study of Torah. In response to this edict, the Sages instituted the reading of passages of Nevi'im that had a thematic relationship to the week's Torah portion. Even today, there is a link, often tenuous but undeniably there, between the [parasha] and the haftarah for the week. [14]

MONDAY/THURSDAY

It is traditional to also read Torah on Mondays and Thursdays, which were the market days in the ancient city of Jerusalem. Robinson explains:

Monday and Thursday were chosen because they were market days in Jerusalem and, therefore, the services were well attended by farmers and merchants from outlying areas. The rabbis also felt it important that there never be more than three days between public Torah readings. The [custom in ancient Palestine] was to read the entire book in three-year cycles, the Babylonian custom in one-year cycles. Eventually, the Babylonian custom prevailed. [15]

So there you have it — the custom was determined by what times were best practically for the Jews to attend. The people didn't come to the reading so much as the reading came to the people. Perhaps this is a concept we would be wise to deeply consider (Someone, write that down!).

ROSH CHODESH (NEW MONTH)

Rosh Chodesh means Head of the Month and is the celebration of the new moon and the new Jewish month it signifies. On every Rosh Chodesh, we read a section from the Book of Numbers, specifically chapter 28 verses 1–15 (with slightly altered readings when this day coincides with Shabbat or other holidays). This section is about the monthly sacrificial offerings.

CHAGGIM (HOLIDAYS)

On different holidays we read corresponding sections of the Torah, and sometimes entire books of the TaNaKh. The following list is a summary of the most notable readings for the most widely observed holidays. Reminder: this list is not exhaustive.

* **ROSH HASHANAH:** In addition to the extensive liturgy, we read Genesis 21–22 which covers the joyous story of Isaac's birth and the chilling story of the Binding of Isaac, AKA the Akedah.
* **YOM KIPPUR:** In addition to the extensive liturgy, we read parts of the Holiness Code and the Book of Jonah.
* **SIMCHAT TORAH:** We read the final chapter of the Book of Deuteronomy and the first chapter of the Book of Genesis.
* **SUKKOT:** We read the Book of Ecclesiastes.
* **CHANUKAH:** We read various sections from the Book of Zechariah.
* **PURIM:** We read the Book of Esther. And we don't only read it, we put on wacky plays called Purim shpiels to tell the story in extra entertaining ways.
* **PASSOVER:** In addition to reading the particular version of the story of the exodus as it appears in our Haggadah (as well as other snippets of texts in the Haggadah that are taken from

Torah, like the four questions), we read Song of Songs.

* SHAVUOT: We read the Book of Ruth.
* TISHA B'AV: We read the Book of Lamentations.

LIFE CYCLE EVENTS

When people are born, become bar, bat, b'nai, b-mitzvah,[16] get married or die, Torah is there. Whether it is reciting psalms at a funeral or while sitting shmira (guarding the body of the deceased) or quoting Song of Songs while exchanging rings under the chuppah (wedding canopy), words of Torah hold our rituals together.

PRAYER

Some of the prayers we say are words taken directly from the Torah or are inspired by Torah. Here are just a few examples:

* Shema including V'ahavta are taken (in part) from the Book of Deuteronomy.
* Mi Chamocha comes from the Song of the Sea, when Miriam leads the Israelites through the Sea of Reeds.
* When Miriam is struck down with leprosy in the Book of Numbers/Bamidbar, Moses prays to God saying, *El na refana la!* Heal her, please! We sing these words today to pray for healing.
* Mah Tovu comes from the blessing of Balaam who tries to curse the Israelites (at the request of The King of Moab, Balak) but seems to only be able to utter praise.
* The Book of Psalms is ripe for the picking when looking for some good prayers to say or quote.
* The Kaddish that we read or chant (either in memory of those who have died or to offer more generic praise to God) was

originally written as a prayer to honor teachers in the beit midrash (study hall). It is a prayer whose original context was Torah study.

TALMUD

Many people (most concentratedly, Orthodox men) study Talmud every day. This is called studying daf yomi. If you read a page of Talmud each day, you will complete the entire Talmud in seven years and sync up with Jews doing the same thing all across the world. At the advent of the most recent cycle, many more folks (who are not Orthodox men) took up this practice. Talmud can be quite intimidating and requires great skill to navigate, but today there are so many resources, including easily accessible translations, to make this practice available to all.

LET'S TALK ABOUT "GOD"

In truth, there is no God-seeking because there is nothing where one could not find Him. How foolish and hopeless must one be to leave one's way of life to seek God: even if one gained all the wisdom of solitude and all the power of concentration, one would miss Him.

— Rabbi Milton Steinberg [17]

There is no quality that space has in common with the essence of God. There is not enough freedom on the top of the mountain; there is not enough glory in the silence of the sea. Yet the likeness of God can be found in time, which is eternity in disguise.

— Rabbi Abraham Joshua Heschel [18]

God is not a short-order cook. — Anne Lamott [19]

God wasn't in the curriculum. Maybe it was assumed that in discussing the Ten Commandments and other topics required for fourth grade Hebrew school we would inevitably get to God — at the very least with the first and second commandments. But there I was, on my own journey of divine discovery (enrolled at Divinity School and dabbling in theological daydreams), and, gosh darn it, I was going to bring God up. By name. I wasn't planning to tell my students what to believe. I wasn't going to try to define the undefinable. I planned to present them with stories and texts showing different dimensions of The Infinite. I was genuinely curious about what these elementary schoolers had to say. What was God to them? Where did they first learn about it? Have they experienced God? I went to tell the religious school director about my plans for several classes to truly delve into this bottomless discussion. She advised caution. I think her fear was that my lesson would become dogmatic — that these kids from Reform Jewish progressive households might go home sounding, well, religious. I noted her advice but proceeded full steam ahead.

After years of reflection, I wonder if the hesitancy around teaching about this topic did not come from the topic, but from the word: God. In so many ways the word God cuts us off from Torah and spirit and ourselves. It is like a check you can't cash. An egg you can't catch without it cracking and splattering all over the place. It tries to do too much.

And then sometimes I hesitate before mentioning God out of fear of being assumed to be anti-intellectual, or worse. Maybe that says more about our current cultural moment, my own baggage, the history of how this word has been used and abused, and where I live in the San Francisco Bay Area, than it does about God.

You know, for the first time I actually feel sorry for this word. We ask it to carry perhaps more than it was meant to carry. We judge it before we meet it, and the truth is that the concept of God was never meant to be held by just three little letters. It's like looking up at the night sky and only seeing one star. Pinched off. Smogged in. Sitting in traffic. Though God is the most popular name to put on the name tag, in the Jewish tradition, it is not the only name for our Eternal Source. Arguably, God is not even a Jewish word at all. In a short essay on this very topic, Dr. Rabbi Ismar Schorsch writes:

Judaism is a wellspring that emits an endless profusion of names for God. The Bible contains some 70; rabbinic literature adds another 90 or more and no one as yet has bothered to tally the number added by

Jewish mystics. As Gershom Scholem wrote more than a half-century ago: "In the last resort, the whole of the Torah [for the author of the Zohar] is nothing but the one great and holy Name of God." [20]

While this chapter does not intend to serve as an exhaustive catalog or analysis of the various sacred names Jewish tradition includes, it does wish to shake up your assumptions. In Jewish tradition (TaNaKh, Talmud, liturgy, folklore, etc.) there is undoubtedly a focus on God as King, Lord, or other designation of patriarchal power. But this is not the whole story.

Before we dig in, a note on why it matters: there is no Torah without the character called God and there is no God without our conceptions of God. We attempt to describe God and understand God. We try to translate God's likeness into language and are always left unsatisfied. A Sisyphusian feeling. An asymptote. Consider the following thought by Rabbi Leon Morris about how our current moment engages with Jewish theology as a sort of poetry:

For many of us, contemporary theology is less about what we know to be true and more about religious ways of organizing and conceiving the world. If medieval and modern Jewish theology were prose, ours is a theology of poetry. In our time, 'doing theology' is far more about meaning and elegance than a truth that ultimately lies beyond our capacity to understand. [21]

Whether you agree with Rabbi Morris or not about the project of contemporary theology, his point is well taken that theology concerns itself with meaning and ways we conceive of the world. So, how we understand God changes how we conceive of the Torah and prayer and, really, anything. With this chapter, I'm not trying to show you the true names of God as if I'm an archaeologist who has finally uncovered the Ark of the Covenant (call Indiana Jones!). Instead, I'm trying to share some theological poetry with you. As such, please enjoy learning about these four names of God that I have curated for us to reflect upon.

HAMAKOM, THE PLACE

We begin with a story of Jacob camping out in the wilderness.

Jacob awoke from his sleep and said, "Surely Adonai is present in this place, and I did not know it!" Shaken, he said, "How awesome is this place! This is none other than the abode of God, and that is the gateway to heaven." [22]

The gateway to heaven, huh? Where is this? After much rabbinic debate as to where this place is, a new name emerges. Let's turn back to our friend Dr. Rabbi Ismar Schorsch to tell us how it happened:

[The following is a] lesson taught by Rabban Gamliel not long after the Roman victory in 70 C.E.: "Why did God choose to reveal Himself to Moses in a lowly burning bush? To make the point that there is no place on earth which is devoid of God's presence." In time Rabban Gamliel's view became concretized in a bold new name for God, perhaps my favorite, HaMakom, which we might render best as "the All-encompassing One." The term expands beyond measure the indeterminate "place," "makom," of Genesis. God is now dauntingly conceived as the space in which the universe exists. [23]

This name, HaMakom, The Place, can be understood as an utterly immanent sacred essence. An eternal presence. It is the name which we use when comforting mourners:

May HaMakom comfort you among the rest of the mourners of Zion and Jerusalem.

HaMakom is a challenge to the thingness of many names of God. Place is expansive. Place is context. And while in our physical world, places are sectioned off and carved up by walls or barbed wire or natural boundaries or lines on maps, HaMakom is the sense that wherever you go, you are still there within the divine presence. You are never lost. HaMakom draws itself around you — a divinity you can live in. HaMakom is the womb you can never leave.

M'KOR MAYIM CHAIM, THE FOUNTAIN OF LIVING WATERS

We learn of The Fountain of Living Waters in the Book of Jeremiah.[24] Fountain can also be translated as spring. But before we get into the imagery of the fountain, let's focus on the water. In the first story of the entire Torah, we read about water. To be more specific, we learn about water within the first two verses:

In the beginning, God created the heavens and the earth — the earth was formless and void, with darkness over the surface of the deep and a wind from God sweeping over the water — [25]

Wait a minute, *what* water? Where did this water come from? The text suggests that this water precedes God's work of creation — precedes God's famous words, *Let there be light*. Water may have been some of the original material with which The Fountain played when starting to make the Earth.

We all know we need water to survive. We all know so much of our material reality and being is water itself. It is not enough to drink water once and quench our thirst; we must drink and drink and drink again. And when we eliminate water from our bodies, it cleans us out. Water swims through us continuously.

The Fountain is not the waters but the place from which they flow. The energy that moves them. The organizing principle. The channel.

What would a Fountain of Living Water look like if it nourished all life? The Fountain organizes the flow of water. Through this flow we are connected to all other life forms — both flora and fauna. Through this flow and its eternal cycle we connect through time and space with generations past. Did I just drink the same molecules that were present in ancient Babylon? Were the tears I cried today in the Atlantic Ocean when my ancestors sailed across in 1923? What tree will the waters in my veins sustain in 1,000 years? The Fountain of Living Water.

EHYEH ASHER EHYEH, I AM THAT I AM

First, some background. Moses has just encountered the burning bush (a bush that is completely on fire but not consumed, from which God calls out) and is talking to God. Moses is asking lots of questions and being a little stiff-necked, if I do say so myself, when suddenly he asks God to tell him God's name.

Moses said to God, "When I come to the Israelites and say to them, 'The God of your fathers' [house] has sent me to you,' and they ask me, 'What is [God's] name?' What shall I say to them?"

And God said to Moses, "Ehyeh-Asher-Ehyeh," continuing, "Thus shall you say to the Israelites: 'Ehyeh sent me to you.'"

And God said further to Moses, "Thus shall you speak to the Israelites: Adonai, the God of your fathers' [house] — the God of Abraham, the God of Isaac, and the God of Jacob — has sent me to you:

This shall be My name forever,
This My appellation for all eternity. [26]

So here, God introduces Godself as *I Am*, and arguably simultaneously as *I Will Be*. How splendid for I Am's name not to be a noun but a phrase — nay, a sentence! I Am. A statement of being. In motion. By that I mean, because it has a subject, I, and a verb, am, there is a sense of aliveness. To put it another way, God did not say God's name was *Being* or *Beingness*. I Am's name is not a state or concept of being. I Am is *in* the action of being. Still and moving at once. Past, present, and future.

What is most fabulous about this name is what happens when you say it out loud. I Am. When we say it, we become the subject. It is a phrase we use liberally each day. I am this or that. I am hungry. I am itchy. I am grateful. It is a name that begs us to try it on. It makes us wonder if, in a way, we too are not some version of I Am. How could we not be?

First Ram Dass and then RuPaul have proclaimed that people are simply God in drag. We only dress ourselves up as something other than our truth–we only pretend we aren't connected to all parts of creation. There has been much made of this name of God both in and out of the Jewish world, and across time up until today. You should look it up and see what you think. For now I leave you with this name that breaks language conventions and the barrier between something out there and something in here. I Am.

SHEKHINAH, THE DIVINE INDWELLING PRESENCE

The Shekhinah is most known for being the feminine presence of God. Foundational Jewish Feminist thinker, scholar, and writer Judith Plaskow describes Shekhinah as the presence with which we can be in relation:

While in the Talmud and midrash the Shekhinah represented the manifest presence of God without any suggestion that this presence was female, in Kabbalism the Shekhinah became a feminine element in God alongside the masculine, "Holy One, Blessed be He"... The Shekhinah, as opposed to the totally unknowable Kadosh Barukh Hu (holy one, blessed be he), is precisely that aspect of God with which we can be in relation, and it is experienced in joint study, community gatherings, lovemaking, and other moments of common and intimate human connection. [27]

Shekhinah is the indwelling presence of God. It is the dwelling that happens within a community and between people. When we engage over words of Torah, the Shekhinah descends and dwells with us.

R. Hananiah ben Teradion said... If two sit together and there are words of Torah [spoken] between them, then the Shekhinah abides among them. [28]

When we share a beautiful Shabbat meal, She descends.

There is a lot more Kabbalistic complexity that I'm missing here, but what is unique about this face of God is not only that She is the sacred feminine. What is unique is that She joins us when we join each other. She is not the one you seek out alone, on a long walk in nature (although maybe She is, who am I to say?). Rather She's the one who sanctifies the love shown between people.

The Shekhinah is sometimes called Daughter and sometimes Sister and here she is called Mother and she is indeed all of these.[29]

She, Herself, is in many relationships — She blesses our relationships. That feeling around the fire, staying out late with friends telling stories. Electricity on the dance floor. She fills in the cracks — She bridges the spaces between us until we are one.

✳✳✳

As you read Torah, consider how all the names of God are metaphors. Consider how each name of God is just an angle of an infinitely dimensional concept. Focusing on only a few angles and neglecting others shuts us off from the greater poem.

And if all else fails, just say HaShem, the name for God which simply means, The Name. At the end of the day, all this language is an approximation. Yes, even in Hebrew. Perhaps Emily Dickinson captures the limits of language best with just four lines:[30]

Could mortal lip divine
The undeveloped Freight
Of a delivered syllable
'Twould crumble with the weight.

TORAH IS A THING

ODE TO A SEFER TORAH

With books, readers skip around, they leave out chapter 3 and go straight to chapter 9, they don't bother remembering the beginning because they can always go back and see what happened, they only read the exciting parts and miss the important parts, they skip to the end. With scrolls, readers have no choice but to be diligent, they have to read carefully, they have to remember the beginning when they reach the end, they can't be fools.

— Dara Horn from *Eternal Life* [31]

By today's standards, a sefer Torah is quite radical. It takes the better part of a year to write and it is written by hand, using all organic materials. Quills from feathers and ink from the earth. Parchment and wood. It is written to last hundreds of years. If it needs repair, we repair it, but there are no updates–no new models made better or faster or brighter or lighter or slimmer or trendier. No words may be added or taken away. It's used often and deeply cherished the more it ages. And when eventually it wears too thin, we bury it. Return it to the source as we do our loved ones. Completely compostable. *Dust you are and to dust you will return.* [32]

A sefer Torah has 304,805 letters. Each one is lovingly sung as it's penned by a scribe (sofer/soferet). When we read it on Monday, Thursday, Shabbat, Rosh Chodesh, chaggim, or any other occasion, we chant.

The trope punctuates.

Then there is Hebrew. This boxy, adorned alphabet is art in and of itself. The same markings our forebears sang. The same sacred decorations that crown certain letters are those that inspired our Sages and were portals for the imagination. Even if you can't read it, you can feel it.

And if you have ever witnessed a child becoming b-mitzvah, you may have seen The Book pass down from generation to generation. L'dor v'dor. In a line of family, the elders stand to one end and imagine that those who passed the Torah to them are by their side, stretching in a line all the way back to Miriam, Moses, and Aaron — the first to receive the Torah directly from The Source. And then the elders pass the scroll to their children, and on and on through the line until it reaches the student. Beyond this emergent adult, the future stands. An entire civilization is in their hands now.

Will they open it? Do they care? We hope we have taught them well, but of course, we have erred. How could we not? But for all our failings and fears — even with all the pain and struggle — we do have kids because life is ultimately good, says the Jew. To be alive is a miracle. Torah tells us to *Choose life!*[33] And we do. We pass it on to our children and hope they will do the same.

As the Torah service progresses and family and friends are invited up by their Hebrew names to receive the honor of an aliyah (saying the blessing before and after chanting Torah), we pause, with the Torah open, to pray for healing. With the Torah open, our prayers are amplified. With the Torah open, we ask the Divine Source of Life that has sustained us to sustain our loved ones and relationships and communities.

The reading is done and the magbiah lifts the Torah so the words are facing us. These words belong to the community, not just the leaders.

Everyone should see them. We stand and raise our pinkies, wrapped in tzitzit, to show that we too, are lifting the Torah. We, too, are responsible for sustaining Jewish life.

And then on Simchat Torah, we unroll the whole thing amongst the community. Little fingers hold the old letters in midair. We see that the text is a cycle — you have to go through the whole thing. *How do you know where you are in the story?* they ask. There are no pages and no numbers. You know where you are by the narrative, or the laws being shared, or the unique configuration of the Hebrew. You know where you are because you have done this before, year after year. Practiced, like learning to tell time on a clock. Torah is analog. Acoustic.

In a world where the newest thing with the longest battery life is of highest value, a sefer Torah challenges us. A sefer Torah is an ancient thing that we use. And while it seems like it might more accurately fit into the category of sculpture or art — that it should be put behind glass in a museum and revered from afar — it is not. It is the most sacred object of the community and it is held to our chests.

As beloved poet Marge Piercy writes in her poem, *Meditation before reading Torah*:

We are the people of the book
and the letters march busy as ants
Carrying the work of the ages through our minds.

We are the people of the book.
Through fire and must and dust we have borne our scrolls tenderly as a baby swaddled in a blanket,
traveling with our words sewn in our clothes
and carried on our backs.
Let us take up the scroll of Torah

and dance with it and touch it
and read it out, for the mind
touches the word and makes it light.
So does light enter us, and we shine.[34]

When a sefer Torah emerges from the ark, and the people rise, there is a pause of awe. After all this time and turmoil and revolution, such a thing lives.

THE TREE OF LIFE

[Wisdom] is a tree of life to those who grasp her,
And whoever holds on to her is happy.

— Proverbs 3:18

Trees are a big deal. They are a big deal for our planet and diet and when we need to set up a tire swing. But in the Torah, trees are a really, *really* big deal. The Garden of Eden is famously home to the Tree of Knowledge of Good and Evil and the Tree of Life. One bears fruit that opens the eyes of Adam and Eve. The other, if eaten from, would bring eternal life. Delicious!

Then God caused to sprout from the ground every tree that was desirable to look at and good for food. Now the Tree of Life was in the middle of the garden, and also the Tree of Knowledge of Good and Evil. [35]

Behold, the man has become like one of Us, knowing good and evil. So now, in case he stretches out his hand and takes also from the Tree of Life and eats and lives forever. [36]

And then later in the text, we are told how to care for and revere particularly young fruit trees.

When you come into the land and have planted all kinds of trees for food, you are to consider their fruit as forbidden. For three years it will be forbidden to you. It is not to be eaten. Then in the fourth year all its fruit will be holy, for giving praise to Adonai. In the fifth year you may eat its fruit. So it will yield its increase to you. [37]

Rabbi Yochanan ben Zakkai said… If you have a sapling in your hand, and someone says to you that the Messiah has come, stay and complete the planting, and only then go out to greet the Messiah. [38]

One of our four new years' days is the birthday of the trees, Tu B'Shevat. We count a tree's years like it's a young child so that we know when they are old enough, strong enough, and healthy enough to offer their fruit. As babies, they are still establishing themselves and need all the energy they can muster to put down roots, fight off infection or pests, and grow. If we harvest their produce too early, we can stifle their growth or hurt their chances of long-term development. We are in a relationship with trees — we take care of them and they will take care of us.

The Torah itself is also considered a tree. Eytz Chaim. The Tree of Life. Specifically, we call the wooden post parts of a sefer Torah the atzei chaim, but in truth, the entire sense of what Torah is is seen through this metaphor of a tree. Why?

In his daily reflections as he works through every single chapter of TaNaKh, Rabbi Amichai Lau-Lavie teaches that the Tree of Life as a concept is *Directly related to Ashera, the Mother Goddess of Canaan, often depicted as a tree.*[39] He continues:

Archaeological discoveries reveal that [Ashera] was worshiped widely, often alongside her husband — YHWH Himself… The poles we use today to handle the Torah scrolls are also known as "trees of life," perhaps a wink to the ancient pillars and posts cherished upon the altars, where the sacred stories were blessed by Her eternal presence?

Perhaps our atzei chaim call into our memory a past goddess, lost to patriarchal domination. But even if this is so, why a tree? Why is the tree such a potent symbol?

A tree starts from a seed. The seed nestles into the ground, and with water, nutrients, and sunlight the seed can sprout. It grows down, deep towards the center of the Earth and also up toward the sky until it pokes its little head out into the fresh air. It grows over time in all directions — the thickness of the trunk, the fullness of the leaves, and the firmness of the roots. Some trees change dramatically depending on the season. Some, not so much. But all continue to bear more and more seeds.

Trees convert carbon dioxide into oxygen to support animal life. They take our waste and recycle it. They filter the Ruach Elohim, the wind/spirit of God.

Trees are homes to life big and small — ants, moss, squirrels, birds. Trees give shelter while they stand, and in new ways after they have fallen. Decay brings new life. Fungi. Bugs. From their pieces, we build homes and tables and chess boards.

We fill our bellies with their produce. Create culture from their flavors. Celebrate the exodus with their sugars. Dates in Morocco. Apples for the Ashkenazi.

So how is Torah like a tree?

Trees renew themselves and add new layers over the years. So too with Torah. When you dig into their core you have a detailed record of an entire life. So too with Torah. After years and years, trees can still bear new, ripe, young fruit. So too with Torah. Some branches survive and strengthen and some crack and fall to the ground. So too with Torah. Trees are an entire ecosystem — the universe in miniature. So too with Torah.

When you eat from the Tree of Life, you live forever. So too with Torah.

After we chant from the Torah we say, *Blessed are You, Eternal One, our God, Sovereign of the world, Who has given us a Torah of truth, and planted in our midst eternal life.*

Planted in our midst. Eternal life. Amen.

FACES

A wise person hears one word and understands two.
— Yiddish Proverb

Each one of us has a face. Each one of us has many faces. We reconfigure our faces into different shapes and angles to communicate different emotions and circumstances. And our faces have changed. The faces we were born with have grown and stretched and perhaps begun to sag. Wrinkles like wood grain. Toothless childhood grins. Dentures in elders. Noses. Mustaches (let's be real, every single person has at least a tiny mustache). Our faces have been scarred or operated upon, by design or not. Our faces have been burned and tanned. Skin sloughed off. Zits. Moles and freckles and other polka dots. Chapped lips. Red sticky lip-glossed lips. Tears and running mascara. Our muscles have burned from too much laughter and strained with too much faking. The dynamic faces we wear and embody are more like our signatures than fingerprints. Each day, a little different.

The Torah, too, has faces. Seventy faces.[40] Each one as complex and alive as our own. What does this mean?

I imagine a seventy-sided die. When you look only at one face of the die, you can't see the others but your community can. No image of Torah is clear or complete without multiple perspectives, cooperation, and communication. You might try to spin the die quickly to examine each side on your own, but as you do the expressions change. In this way, (at least) seventy faces of Torah.

Then I imagine the same die, only this time it is rolled and lands with one side facing up. That is the face for the generation — until it is rolled again. All possible understandings of Torah are already present, we just don't know them yet. We haven't met them yet. And then, if we roll the die and it lands on a side we've seen before, *ahh*, we get to meet it in a new time — that too will be different. Seeing a friend after years apart. Coming home from a long trip.

But what if the seventy faces of Torah are actually resting, one on top of the other — each in a slightly different tone or vibrating at a slightly different frequency? Collaging with tissue paper or mixing a record. A photo that has been double exposed. Layers. You can experience all of them at once, but in another sense, you cannot. That would be stimulation overload. We can only focus on so much at one time. When you're specifically asked to look for things that are blue, it's more challenging to notice things that are yellow. The limits of human processing.

The Torah teaches that when Moses was overwhelmed and unable to hold all the responsibility of his position, God told him to gather seventy elders for support — to share the burden.

I will draw upon the spirit that is on you and put it upon them; they shall share the burden of the people with you, and you shall not bear it alone.[41]

Perhaps Torah needs this sort of plurality to bear itself — to bear us. It is not that we might apply various approaches to Torah (although that is also true), but that Torah itself is like this community of elders, sharing the burden of the people.

HONEY UNDER YOUR TONGUE

Honey might be all the evidence we need that life is good. Imagine this: a bee takes flower nectar, regurgitates it to another bee, who then passes it on to another bee, etc. And then finally, a bee stores this already-been-chewed-pre-honey, speeds up the evaporation process, and seals it up. Boom! Honey! (Disclaimer: I may have misrepresented the science a bit but I am in fact not a scientist and the preceding was mostly to create a metaphor which you will encounter shortly.) There are few things that naturally occur in our world as majestic as honey. There are few things as sweet, for sure. It is no wonder then that honey became a symbol for the words of Torah.

In our epic biblical love poem, Shir HaShirim, we read, *Milk and honey are under your tongue.*[42] Whose tongue? My tongue? In the commentary, it is explained as follows:

Honey and milk: The allusion is to the two modalities of Torah (written and oral) and the fact that the Shekhinah is situated between the two cherubim.[43]

Your lips drip: [With] explanations of Torah.[44]

And then in the Psalms, we get this metaphor again:

The precepts of God are... sweeter than honey, than drippings of the comb.[45]

Finally, in the Book of Ezekiel, we get a vision of literally eating the sweet scroll of the Torah. No wonder Ezekiel is known for his wackadoo prophecies.

God said to me, "Mortal, eat what is offered to you; eat this scroll, and go speak to the House of Israel." So I opened my mouth, and God gave me this scroll to eat, as God said to me, "Mortal, feed your stomach and fill your belly with this scroll that I give you." I ate it, and it tasted as sweet as honey to me. Then God said to me, "Mortal, go to the House of Israel and repeat My very words to them."[46]

The Torah doesn't taste sour like lemons. It doesn't taste bitter like coffee. It doesn't taste salty like lox. It doesn't taste umami like whatever the heck tastes umami. Torah is sweet like honey.

And this idea does not remain metaphorical. In many Jewish communities, it is traditional for kids to lick honey off of a surface on which Hebrew letters have been written. This might happen the first time a student learns Hebrew, or maybe even at the beginning of each school year. A dear friend and colleague gives her students Mike and Ikes* *whenever* they read Torah. The idea is to associate learning Torah with sweetness — the words themselves are a treat.

While I can't comment on the success of it, I've always loved this practice. Admittedly, I even have a fondness for its evolution into candy-throwing when a student becomes b-mitzvah. What other subject area actively encourages its practice to be enjoyable and even sweet? I certainly did not receive treats when I learned my times tables. As a pedagogical strategy, well done, Jewish tradition!

But what does it mean that the words of Torah are honey? Wouldn't a more nutritionally substantial metaphor be stronger? Like, bread? It is true that milk comes into the metaphor often, as seen above, but it is the honey that really sticks out. And of course, we don't give kids a glass of milk the first time they learn the aleph bet (although we do give them ice cream on Shavuot to commemorate the giving of the Torah at Mt. Sinai/Horeb, and there are some great interpretations for why we do that — look them up!). So, why honey? Besides being sweet, is there another reason?

When I think about the words of the Torah themselves, I can't help but think about some of the horrifically violent plot points involving evil characters or mass death. Surely those parts don't taste like honey. Or what about the extremely dull ritualistic parts? Honey doesn't come to mind then either.

No, it's not that the substance of what Torah says is always gooey goodness. It is partly the satisfaction and joy that come from study. How sweet it feels to know you are growing wiser. But Kohelet takes it one step further.

To the person, namely, who pleases God, God has given the wisdom and shrewdness to enjoy themselves.[47]

This text implies that it takes wisdom to be able to enjoy ourselves. It is wise to proclaim that life is good. It may even be wise to indulge a little! In other words, it is not just the process of becoming wise that tastes like honey, but that wisdom should be used to find the honey.

Our tradition says that if you don't enjoy yourself adequately, you will be called upon to explain yourself.

R. Chizkiyah said in the name of Rav: You will one day give a reckoning for everything your eyes saw which, although permissible, you did not enjoy.[48]

Let us end where we began. It is curious that bees have to pass the flower nectar amongst each other before it can be transformed into honey. Did the ancients know this is how it worked? Maybe through study, and sharing the contents of our mouths (as words), we turn the nectar of potential into the honey of wisdom. When we give kids honey as they begin their studies, we are giving the blessing: may you too turn these words into divine sugar.

FIRE ON FIRE

How was the Torah written? It was written with letters of black fire on a surface of white fire. — Midrash Tanchuma Bereshit 1

When I think about fire I think about cooking. Starting the stove or building a campfire. I think about transformation. Boiling water turns an egg firm and a potato soft. Fire is a doorway to change. Too much fire is a burnt marshmallow.

The second thing I think about is fire-activated seeds. While forest fires can devastate entire ecosystems, including human communities, there are also some seeds that need to be in touch with fire in order to germinate. In a National Forest Foundation essay on the effects of fire on trees, Luba Mullen writes the following:

The actual seeds of many plants in fire-prone environments need fire, directly or indirectly, to germinate. These plants produce seeds with a tough coating that can lay dormant, awaiting a fire, for several years. Whether it is the intense heat of the fire, exposure to chemicals from smoke or exposure to nutrients in the ground after fire, these seeds depend on fire to break their dormancy.[49]

Fire can break a seed's dormancy. Wake it up. Waking up is itself a sort of transformation. Jewish tradition teaches that when we wake up after sleeping, it is as if our soul has returned to our body. When we sleep, our soul goes off and mingles with other souls, or maybe just sits somewhere and catches up on the crossword. At that time, our soul is not in our body — there is a separation. And then every morning the first words we are taught to say are:

I offer thanks to You, Eternal Source of Life, for You have mercifully restored my soul within me.

To wake up, in one expression of the Jewish imagination, is to be re-ensouled. To be reunited is to be transformed, in a sense.

The third thing I think about when I think about fire: Shabbat candles. Striking the match. Striking the second match when the first one doesn't work. That initial smell of smoke. Running my finger through the flame the way I learned at some family dinner from some family member, many years ago. It was such a thrill that I could touch fire. Touch it! But only in passing.

The fourth thing I think about is motion. Fire is always moving because it is always burning something. Whether pine needles or propane, fire needs fuel.

It is taught that the Torah is fire on fire. The black fire of the Hebrew crackles upon the white fire of the page beneath.

Rebbi Phineas in the name of Rebbi Simeon ben Laqish: The Torah which the Holy One, Praise to God, gave to Moses, was white fire engraved in black fire. It was fire mixed with fire; hewn from fire, given from fire. That is what is written: From God's right hand, the fiery law to them.[50]

If this is so, what is the fuel? What is being woken up or transformed? How can we relate to it without getting burned?

One of the most famous fires inside of the Torah is of course that of the burning bush:

There the angel of God appeared to [Moses] in flames of fire from within a bush. Moses saw that, though the bush was on fire, it did not burn up. So Moses thought, "I will go over and see this strange sight — why the bush does not burn up." [51]

It was strange to Moses that the fuel (the bush) was not being consumed. Strange enough that it caught his attention and drew him closer to the Divine Presence. The strange sight succeeded in capturing his attention and bringing him near, but he was also not supposed to come *too* near. A voice from the bush tells him to stop when he approaches too close. So what is the fuel of the fires of Torah? We might think of the fuel like that of the bush–the presence of a divine messenger. The visible fires of the Hebrew and the page mean that a deeper source — a divine message — exists. Fire does not sustain itself without fuel.

Now we will discuss the transformative powers of fire. What is the fire of Torah waking up or transforming? The obvious answer is the reader. As we run our minds through the ancient flickers of wisdom, like the seed, we prepare ourselves to grow. Something melts away or softens or strengthens or whistles inside of us. And like the soul returning to the body upon waking from sleep, there is a spiritual awakening that happens when a student reunites with the generative heat of Torah. We move from being asleep to being awake to being Torah-awake — an elevated state.

And when might the fire of Torah burn us? As with passing a finger through a Shabbos candle or Moses approaching the burning bush, there is an important boundary to hold. If we stay too long inside of Torah — if we make our aim to climb between the letters and never emerge — we will be charred to a crisp. Ultimately, Torah is to be lived outside of its pages.

The black-and-white fire of Torah is not a destination in and of itself.

Instead, these fires are calls to action. If we remain inside the world of Torah too much — if we only learn and never apply — we die. Torah is precisely intended for the opposite.

You shall keep My laws and My rules, by the pursuit of which human beings shall live.[52]

I gave them My laws and taught them My rules, by the pursuit of which a human being shall live.[53]

Torah is a passageway. Torah is a transformation. Torah is for the sake of life.

MELODY AND MEANING

Towards the end of the Book of Deuteronomy we read one of the most game-changing verses in the entire Torah. It is the line that leads to majority rule in the story of The Oven of Akhnai (Which you can read in the chapter entitled, What Does 'Judaism' Say About This?). It is the line that takes Jewish law and practice out of the hands of God and places it, squarely, in the mouths and hearts of the people. And while this following passage invites us to interpret the meaning of Torah for ourselves, it also gives us a window into how, whether we try to or not, we are constantly interpreting the form of Torah. Let's start with the original text:

Surely, this Instruction [mitzvah] which I enjoin upon you this day is not too baffling for you, nor is it beyond reach. It is not in the heavens, such that you would say, 'Who among us can go up to the heavens and get it for us and impart it to us, that we may observe it?' Neither is it beyond the sea, that you should say, 'Who among us can cross to the other side of the sea and get it for us and impart it to us, that we may observe it?' No, the thing is very close to you, in your mouth and in your heart, to observe it.[54]

What does this last line mean? In my mouth? Really?

A French Medieval commentator known by the acronym Rashi says that this has to do with how Torah is transmitted: *No, the thing is very close to you — the Torah has been given to you in writing and orally.*

Medieval Sephardi Torah commentator Ibn Ezra says this has to do with where the commandments are acted out: *In thy mouth, and in thy heart. For the heart is the core of the commandments. Some commandments require the uttering of statements that serve to reinforce the heart. Others consist of deeds that will lead a person to utter the required statements.*

Torah is in our mouths because that is how we teach it and learn it. Torah is in our mouths because sometimes we have to use our mouths to do the commandments, like saying the Shema.

I'm thinking about how Torah becomes ours the moment we speak it. I'm thinking about all those who cannot speak. Is Torah in their mouths?

When we read a passage of Torah out loud, we can't help but emphasize certain parts, or take breaks when we need a breath, or stumble over unfamiliar words. Even with our incredible musical technology called trope, which standardizes the way we chant Hebrew, each of our voices is different — not to mention that our voices change with age and depending on what we did the night before. And of course, there are multiple versions of trope that can be applied, depending on the time of the week, who you ask, or where you are in the world. When Torah is in our mouths, it can't help but be unique. It's live!

Think about it this way: each time we read or chant Torah we are doing a cover version of it. Like, the original performance was at Mt. Sinai/Horeb. But since then, we have been in an infinite after-party, trying to keep the music going. And every time we play the album, performances are influenced by the individual performers — their preferences, ideas, generation, strengths, and training — as well as the cultural zeitgeist. Some people create punk rock Torah covers, while others are more classical, trying to get back to that original show. Adding to this metaphor, at the end of the Torah the final commandment is to *Write for yourselves this song*.[55] What if we remembered that Torah is a song?

Beyond speaking, any time we think of Torah or hear it or simply copy a piece of text in our own handwriting, that too makes it ours and new. From whom would we have copied the text? Another scribe, perhaps? If we read it to ourselves or experience the text in any way, the voice inside of our heads makes decisions about how it will sound and what will stand out. Our mind takes in the information and makes sense of it only in the way our particular minds can. In our imaginations we perform a cover show. Torah in our mouths means Torah made our own.

When we read Torah, often we do so to consciously interpret its content—to consider how we want to apply Jewish tradition to today. However, if the Torah is in our mouths, it is not so much that our *goal* should be to interpret Torah, but rather that in every single interaction with it, whether fleeting or hunkered down, we can *only* interpret the Torah.

Is this anything more than a classic conversation about form and content? Maybe not. But so often we focus on the content (What does Torah mean?!) and forget the form altogether, as if the words are just vessels for value and aren't themselves sacred. What about the music of Torah?

There is one exceptional example of how the music of a text-the form- has proven even more powerful than the content. I'm referring to Kol Nidre. Kol Nidre is the prayer (more accurately, a legal formulation) we hear and chant on the evening of Yom Kippur—a day many Jews would consider the holiest of the year. This tradition has become so important to the liturgy that we even call the entire service Kol Nidre. Kol Nidre means All Vows and in its original composition, it nullifies all vows one has made from the previous Yom Kippur until the current one. Journalist Michael Weiss succinctly explains the history of this prayer in his essay, T*he Anti-Semite's Favorite Jewish Prayer: The centuries-long controversy over Yom Kippur's Kol Nidre*:

Then, in the 12th century, Meir ben Samuel, the son-in-law of the revered French rabbi Rashi, altered the wording to reflect the year to come, arguing that pre-emptive annulment was more in keeping with the letter and spirit of the Nedarim, the Talmudic treatise on vows. Ben Samuel also added to the prayer the phrase "we do repent [of them all]," which aligned it more closely with the purpose of atonement. His version has been taken up by the bulk of the Ashkenazim, while the Sephardim continue to prefer the older, retroactive one.[56]

This prayer has had a funky history. But wow, has it persevered! In his canonical essay on the topic, *The Curious Case of Kol Nidre*, Herman Kieval writes:

Kol Nidre has had to survive centuries of powerful and persistent opposition, expressed not only by enemies and detractors of Judaism but even by eminent rabbis who have challenged the very principle underlying its recitation — the concept of a blanket annulment of sacred vows.[57]

Why did it live on? Why keep this prayer, considering all of its problems? The generally recognized answer is simple. The music. As an example, Kieval writes:

So well entrenched was the melody used in Prague at the end of the 16th century that the codifier R. Mordecai Jaffe could write: "Most of the text of Kol Nidre, as it is now printed in the Mahzorim, makes no sense and is quite unintelligible; the only thing that gives it substance and meaning is the melody."[58]

It was the music that allowed this prayer to survive the scrutiny of the scholars. The music conveys a meaning that words can't quite capture. A meaning you can feel.

What would it be like to read or chant Torah for this kind of meaning? To enjoy and marvel at yet another cover of our resilient and creative tradition. What if we wrote out an ancient text simply to be in awe of how many times these words have been copied by our eternal community? Each time is different.

There is meaning in the melody.

TORAH IS A TIMEKEEPER

CALENDAR OF STORIES

By now my students are sick of me saying that the Jews belong to the oldest, most repetitive book club in the world. For what it's worth, I still think it's funny. But more importantly, that is one of my favorite ways to make sense of how we read Torah. We read the Torah in its entirety every year, portion by portion, starting right after the High Holidays. Then, when we get to the end, we roll it back up and start again at the beginning. Now that's what I call dedication.

However, there is another way I think about reading the Torah. It is a way for which I have not created a corny joke… yet.

I first noticed it during my second summer working at Camp Tawonga. It was during Shabbat morning Torah services and the young adults who had been assigned to act out the story of that week's Torah portion were getting ready to perform their wacky interpretation of the spies scouting out the Promised Land. This felt all too familiar. It was as if only last year another group of 18-year-olds had acted out this same scene in a similarly chaotic and hilarious fashion wearing boas, bathrobes, and cowboy hats.

But then I thought, of course we heard it last year! Last year we were also reading the Torah mid-June and generally speaking the Book of Numbers is read sometime in June, and the story of the spies is right in the middle of the Book of Numbers. Taking into consideration our lunar/solar hybrid Jewish calendar, the stories don't always line up

with the same dates each year. But each section of the Torah falls into the same season every year.

Oh, we are reading about Sarah? There is a good chance it is early fall. We are entrenched in a litany of laws about sacrifices? I'd bet on April.

Torah is a story unlike any other. Specifically, I am talking about the Five Books of Moses, though, as mentioned earlier, we do read parts of the Prophets regularly too, as they have been paired up with portions as supplemental reading (We call this the haftarah). Torah is a story unlike any other, not only because it tells you how to read it — one section at a time, every week, until the end and then start over — but because in reading it, it tells you where we are in the year. Torah can tell time. We will never collectively read the story of Noah's Ark in March. It's not the time.

Ok, cool party trick. Tell me the date and I'll tell you if Moses is about to hit that rock. Why does this matter? Does this insight change anything for us? We mark time with stories on every holiday. And at Purim and Passover and Chanukah, the story is basically the biggest part. But how does the yearly cycle of stories fit into a larger rhythm?

In fact, the stories we tell at holidays and the cycle of Torah reading enhance one another. In his Days of Awe classic text, *This Is Real and You Are Completely Unprepared*, Rabbi Alan Lew describes this interaction:

The sacred calendar and the year cycle of Torah readings...often rhyme in subtle ways; they use the same language or address the same issues at the same time. Pesach, for example, is the holiday of physical purification. We get down to essentials. We remove all leaven — all flour that has undergone modification and expansion — from our homes and then finally from our bodies. We possess and we eat that which is stale — all the old flour in our possession. And what do we read in the Torah during the weeks when we are preparing for this purification? The laws concerning the cult of purification at the Great Sanctuary in the wilderness.[59]

It's as if we count our year in one continuous story with special anecdotes or tangents for the holidays. Or seen in the opposite way, the holidays are like the big waves — the pivotal moments — and the Torah narrative is the constant watery flow — the current throughout the year. However you see this interaction, it is clear that the Jewish default is to understand time through story. We combine charts — the calendars that hang on our walls — with scrolls. Numbers and narrative. And, of course, in Hebrew, numbers are written with letters.

Turn it, turn it. You can't just tell the story once. Because each time it will be different. No August is the same. You will grow up with the story, as you do with the seasons. Remember your first visit to the snow? Remember when you finally understood that Noah's Ark is horrifically violent and not a story for children? Same text, different you. New meaning to be made.

And finally, this insight sheds light on how we understand time altogether. Time is not only a ticking clock or a trip around the sun. It is the scroll beneath the letters.

WE ALSO READ JOSHUA

Aside from singing and dancing, the big production on Simchat Torah is unrolling and rerolling the Torah. We celebrate the completion of another cycle of reading by, well, reading! We start with V'zot Habracha, the last parasha from the Book of Deuteronomy and then immediately follow that up with a reading from the beginning of Bereshit, the first parasha from the Book of Genesis. Cycles. There is no beginning and there is no end. To everything, turn, turn, turn (The Byrds certainly read Torah). Like the cycles of the moon or the seasons, the scroll winds and winds but never starts or stops.

Except, something else happens on Simchat Torah. We read the first chapter of the Book of Joshua. Joshua is Moses' successor and the leader who will take the Israelites into the Promised Land. The Torah, as in the Five Books of Moses (the scroll we are unrolling and rerolling), ends with the death of Moses. The Book of Joshua starts with just that. The first line is literally, *After the death of Moses*,[60] because there is in fact an after. It doesn't only begin again. The story also continues. The Israelites enter the land. There are new spies who meet a harlot, Rachav. There are Samson and Delilah, Yael with her bloody peg and hammer, David and Goliath, Solomon's temple in Jerusalem, Queens Esther and Vashti, and Daniel who is put into a lion's den. There is so much more to the story! We keep reading further while simultaneously starting over.

This tension between historical and cyclical time is mirrored in the Jewish calendar which is a lunar/solar hybrid. The months are based on the movement of the moon. Each new moon means a new month — Rosh Chodesh. But, in order to keep the seasons and the historical holidays for those seasons in the same place, we have to adjust the calendar so it lines up with the movement of the sun. In *The Jewish Holidays*, Rabbi Michael Strassfeld explains how this works:

The Jewish calendar is basically cyclic in its dependence on the moon. However, it is adjusted at regular intervals to keep the festivals in their proper seasons — e.g., Pesach in the spring. The workings of the calendar with its lunar/solar complexity reflect the mixture of both kinds of time throughout the year. Pesach is cyclic, but it is also historical, for the Exodus was seen by the tradition as a verifiable event.[61]

In other words, our entire sense of the year is a balance between cycles and history. Strassfeld argues that the balance achieved by these two kinds of time is exactly what we need:

We need the process of self-evaluation called forth by historical time to rouse us to change and thus foster creation and progress. Without that, it would be easy to become increasingly sedentary both spiritually and physically as our lives passed us by... On the other hand, we need cyclic time to give us perspective on the dangers of constantly seeking progress due to an unbridled devotion to the movement of historical time... Particularly in our day, the sense of cyclic time is a necessary balance to the pressures in our society to succeed. If historical time teaches us that to be alive is to move, cyclic time teaches us that sometimes to wait in place is more important than moving on.[62]

At this moment of Simchat Torah, we beautifully experience both the cyclic and historical nature of Torah. Torah embodies both versions of time.

All of this talk of balance is making me think about that classic Hasidic teaching from Rabbi Simcha Bunem:

It was said of Reb Simcha Bunem, an 18th-century Hasidic rebbe, that he carried two slips of paper, one in each pocket. One was inscribed with the saying from the Talmud: Bishvili nivra ha-olam, 'for my sake the world was created.' On the other he wrote a phrase from our father Avraham in the Torah: V'anokhi afar v'efer,' 'I am but dust and ashes.' He would take out and read each slip of paper as necessary for the moment.[63]

I am but dust and ashes — seasons come and seasons go — and for my sake the world was created — this is my moment in history. Both thoughts are necessary to regulate our lives. A balance of humility and audacity.

A time for seeking and a time for losing,
A time for keeping and a time for discarding;
A time for ripping and a time for sewing,
A time for silence and a time for speaking.[64]

This balance is Torah.

THERE IS NO TIMELINE IN TORAH

We are not human beings having a spiritual experience; we are spiritual beings having a human experience. — Pierre Teilhard de Chardin

I forget when I first heard the teaching, *There is no timeline in Torah*.[65] Perhaps it was when I was in college and had started attending text study at the UCLA Hillel with all the Orthodox kids. This concept was both freeing and daunting. What does this mean? Surely, Abraham comes before Isaac; considering he is his father, he has to! It's the law of nature. But see, Torah operates by rules all its own. I soon learned, to my delight, that on the one hand, *There is no timeline in Torah* means that all of the characters and plots and laws of the Torah know each other in some strange Twilight Zone dreamlike sort of way. And in the same way, conversations about Torah that were started millennia ago are still as alive as the day they began. What's more, I'm part of them! As Torah becomes timeless, I too become timeless. Just as my physical form is governed by the rules of the physical world — my face is starting to wrinkle and my belly rumbles in hunger — Torah lives on a different plane with different rules. Torah is a playground for my soul. Buckle up. This one is going to get a little groovy.

Now, time is a topic that gets much attention by the 20th century sage, Rabbi Abraham Joshua Heschel, in his masterpiece, *The Sabbath*. In the following passage, Heschel compares the dimensions of time and space as a way of thinking about The Divine.

Time, that which is beyond and independent of space, is everlasting; it is the world of space which is perishing. Things perish within time; time itself does not change. We should not speak of the flow or passage of time but of the flow or passage of space through time. It is not time that dies; it is the human body which dies in time. Temporality is an attribute of the world of space, of things in space. Time which is beyond space is beyond the division of past, present and future...We share time, we own space. Through my ownership of space, I am a rival of all other beings; through my living in time, I am a contemporary of all other beings...It is the dimension of time wherein man meets God, wherein man becomes aware that every instant is an act of creation...Time is the presence of God in the world of space, and it is within time that we are able to sense the unity of all beings.[66]

Of course, Heschel is also talking about Torah. Torah is shared, not owned. Torah is beyond past, present, and future. In Torah, we meet God. In Torah we encounter, not conquer, time. In Torah, we exit a spatial world and enter the reality of the soul, which is eternal.

In a fabulous midrash about the angel Lailah, we are gifted the idea that all souls were created at the start of the universe — meaning, we all have existed and will exist beyond the limits of our physical bodies. The midrash reads:

You should know that every soul, from Adam to the end of the world, was formed during the six days of creation, and that all of them were present in the Garden of Eden and at the time of the giving of the Torah...All the souls that would exist in the future were fashioned with the first man, and they will exist to the end of the world.[67]

It is our souls who are invited into Torah. Our souls escaped from Egypt. Our souls stood at Sinai. Not our bodies but that incredible

God-like part of us that was made in the Image. This body I'm in as I write is quite different from the day I was born. And yet, I have this thing that I call *my life* which has remained. I have cut my hair enough times to know that my material self is always regenerating. It is not this set of cells that was at Sinai but the eternal part of me. It is still there now.

When we comment and question the text, we are in conversation with souls of all times. The conversation expands like the universe does. In their chapter on this topic of time and Torah, Amos Oz and Fania Oz-Salzberger write:

[another Jewish treatment of time] is not linear, not even backward-facing linear. It denies chronology altogether. "There is no early or late in the Torah." The first man to put this principle on record was the Mishnaic Rabbi Eliezer son of Rabbi Jose of Galilee. The big cannons of Jewish exegesis, Rashi included, followed suit. Repeating this phrase in variations, they insisted that the essence of the Torah, original text or sage interpretation, does not belong to any timeline. It is a corpus of pure, perennial truth.[68]

I'm considering now that we ought not to say there is no timeline in Torah but that through Torah we access a purity of time. A time saved from the conventions and principles of our physical world. An uncategorized time. As Heschel muses, this is where we meet the Source of Creation.

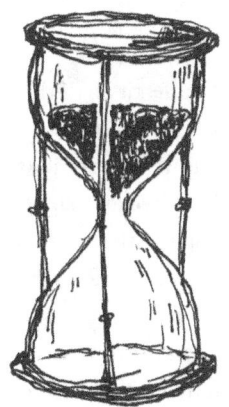

It is our soul's nature to be eternal. We always have been and always will be. Therefore, we can find an affinity context in Torah where we are not bound by our spatial realities. Torah is both a world we build and an entrance to eternity.

MY DAD'S CHUMASH

Did we even have one in the house? I was trying to read the weekly parasha for the first time on my own and found myself completely Torah-less. While studying to become bat mitzvah I had received a siddur, but not a chumash. So, I went on a search in my parents' house for The Book. After quickly glancing at the books in the living room — lined up by color for decorative purposes or large and full of art prints for coffee table purposes — I went downstairs. Now, the books downstairs were a little more serious. These are the books that you want to hold onto but may never read ever again. Classics. Library must-haves. Old versions of the dictionary, collections of poetry and Steinbeck. These were the bookshelves next to which I had been watching TV for years but had never explored. And then, all of a sudden, there it was. On a navy spine, the gold capital letters simply spelled out, THE TORAH. I was pretty sure this was it.

I pulled it off of the shelf and to my surprise, my father's full name was printed in the same gold that was on the cover, WAYNE ELLIS BATAVIA. Did he receive it as a gift? An award maybe? I didn't have to wonder long because right there, on the first page, in blue cursive, someone had written that this book had been presented to my dad by the Sisterhood and Brotherhood of Temple Sinai in Oakland, California on June 5, 1970. This was my father's bar mitzvah chumash. And not to throw my dad under the bus or anything, but it felt like, just maybe, it had never been opened. Perfect, I thought. Brand new and yet charmingly vintage. This will be mine.

Now you might think this chapter is about how I feel connected to my dad through this book, but you'd be only partially correct. I love thinking about my dad at age thirteen, short for his age, blond, and smiling with relief as he received this gift. I imagine him coming home after the celebration and putting this book on a shelf somewhere. Maybe he did open it once or twice. Did he read it? This book must have meant something to him because here it was, some forty-five years later, in my hands.

But, like I said, this is only part of why I feel connected to this chumash. This was also my first chumash. And because it was mine now, I started to do what any English major knows how to do best: annotate. I jumped in with my pencil and started underlining and circling and commenting galore. For the next few years, when I needed a copy of the Torah, this was the one I schlepped around and marked up.

Today I have around eight different versions of the Torah or TaNaKh sitting on my shelf now (yes, Colleen, I do need them all). But this one holds a special something for me. It holds me in it. When I look through the pages, I notice who I was when I first picked up this book. It's like looking at photos of myself from college. There I am, underlining *Now the manna was like coriander seed*[69] or writing *What is "enough?"* next to the laws of shmita in Leviticus 23. It's like reading an old diary. What was I thinking about? What jumped off the page back then? Where was I living and where was I working and how had I slept the night before when I made these marks?

The other day I read the d'var Torah I gave upon becoming bat mitzvah in 2004 at the same Temple Sinai as my father. The parasha was Tetzaveh and the theme I'd chosen to expound upon was sacrifice. I was impressed with how well I understood delayed gratification (arguably better than I do now) and how clear I was about what was right and wrong. I felt like I was meeting myself—teaching myself. Thirteen-year-old me, meet 30-year-old me! It was an experience that both bridged and marked time. Through the text, the day of my bat mitzvah ceremony and the current moment became one. My own private page of Talmud. As if by time-travel-magic, I was studying with my childhood self. *All minds who ever lived are contemporaries.*[70] Even my own.

I still use my dad's chumash sometimes, especially when I want to encounter myself. When I flip through the pages I see myself meeting many of these verses for the first time. I see myself shocked at what I now barely notice. I feel a deepening love for this young Torah nerd, and I'm her.

TORAH IS A RELATIONSHIP

YES, YOU ARE YOUR BROTHER'S KEEPER

The thrill of learning is just this: that you never quite know in advance what's going to happen when you encounter the sacred text through someone else's eyes. — Rabbi Steven Greenberg [71]

Torah is only acquired in community. — Talmud Berakhot 63b

The first babies ever born in the Torah? Maybe you've heard of them: Cain and Abel. Oh, and the first murder was between them, too. We learn of these two in the Book of Genesis when they are born to Adam and Eve as the first humanly conceived and birthed people. After God does not accept Cain's offering and does accept Abel's, Cain kills his brother out in the field. God then asks, *Where is your brother?* to which Cain responds with the infamous question (a rather Jewish moment, I might add), *Am I my brother's keeper?* [72]

Um, duh. If only Cain had learned to study Torah.

I have taught some version of Hebrew school for many years now. While the curriculum changes from synagogue to synagogue and youth group to summer camp, there are some deeply wise pedagogical methods baked into the gigantic Jewish cake of learning. One of the wisest is the method of learning in chevruta. This means studying in a pair or very small group of people. Chevruta is both the name of the model of studying and of the person with whom you are studying. For example, you could say, *Alright class, we are going to get into chevruta for this next text* or *Bernie is my chevruta.* Roughly, chevruta means friend, partner, or fellow.

Our tradition has various texts that speak to the value of studying with others. The Talmud records famous chevruta couples, like Reish Lakish and Rabbi Yochanan ben Zakkai, or Hillel and Shammai (though they might not have referred to themselves as such). What is a chevruta if not an intellectual sparring partner? A person to sharpen your theological and argumentative edges. Jewish tradition teaches that learning with a partner can both strengthen the individual and result in a higher understanding of the text:

Rabbi Ḥama son of Rabbi Ḥanina said: What is the meaning of that which is written: 'Just as iron sharpens iron, so too, a person sharpens the countenance of their friend' (Proverbs 27:17)? This verse comes to tell you that just as with these iron implements, one sharpens the other when they are rubbed against each other, so too, when Torah scholars study together, they sharpen one another in halakha.[73]

Just as fire does not ignite in a lone stick of wood but in a pile of kindling, so too, matters of Torah are not retained and understood properly by a lone scholar who studies by themselves, but by a group of sages.[74]

Chevruta learning is like a Swiss army knife — one thing with many uses. It can help solve legal, moral, or textual problems. It teaches us to hold multiple interpretations. It improves intellectual and spiritual fitness in each learner. It trains learners to thoroughly engage with one another, not just use each other for some other end. Chevruta is a team. The chevruta versus the text. Or, the chevruta and the text versus the issue at hand. We either all succeed together, or not. Chevruta creates a *we*.

In their study of chevruta learning, entitled *A Philosophy of Havruta: Understanding and Teaching the Art of Text Study in Pairs*, Elie Holzer and Orit Kent reflect upon how chevruta study teaches social responsibility and forces learners to learn from each other, not just one centralized authority figure we typically call the teacher.

Instead of only being concerned with what the teacher is saying, [a chevruta learner] is confronted by the need to learn with a fellow student. And instead of only paying attention to her own accomplishments, the chevruta learner is expected to take into account her partner's success as well... the ethical responsibility for one's partner's learning constitutes one of the foundations of interpersonal practices... students learn to challenge their partner's textual interpretation, even when they agree, in order to help their partner refine and improve the quality of the interpretation.[75]

This is precisely the opposite of how I felt growing up. In high school, while we were frequently assigned group projects, nine out of ten times the strategy was either divide and conquer, see you at presentation day, or two kids took the lead and rest kind of putzed around in the background (you know who you are). I'll admit right here and now, I didn't care that much what my classmates had to say. My goal was to get the best grade I could and almost no part of that required me to listen. As long as my teacher heard me say something smart in each class so I could get my participation credit, things would be okay. Definitely not the chevruta model. Then, when I got to college and started taking English literature seminars, I noticed just how much people loved to dunk on each other. *Oh, you haven't read Proust?* Sure, our papers weren't graded on a curve like those kids over in the sciences, but the spirit of competition and stench of smug self-congratulatory arrogance was alive and well. There were winners and losers in this zero-sum game. Not so for chevruta learning:

> [Chevruta learning] should also help to nurture and cultivate the student's awareness and ability to care about, empathize with, and assist another person in her or his own learning process. When the student perceives the scope is his responsibility to include a genuine care for the learning of his partner, and when this deep concern translates itself into concrete solicitousness and effective assistance, the student is said to enact the ethical-relational dimension of chevruta text study.[76]

Of course, chevruta learning has competitive elements—a learner might feel competitive with their partner at any time throughout the study time, or with themselves to beat whatever would be the Torah equivalent of their personal record. Competition isn't all bad—it can be quite motivating! However, the *end* goal isn't who can get the best grade or their foot in the door for that internship. The end goal actually varies depending on the reason for studying. It is not prescribed by the teacher and due at 3:05 PM. It is decided upon by the chevruta, in cooperative partnership. Are we trying to solve a textual problem? Are we trying to decide how to proceed with a certain ritual or law? Are we working out our minds and delighting in the sparks that fly? This kind of collaborative learning isn't just a breath of fresh air from our American educational norms (at least, as I've experienced them), it is something else entirely. It puts learning in the hands of the learners. Co-op learning.

The only way this sort of learning can take root is if, at the end of the day, each learner isn't judged by their own individual achievements, but instead, by how they were able to bring along their teammates. It doesn't matter if they learn while their partner doesn't.[77] This is a radical departure from a strain of American culture that preaches *primarily* personal responsibility with charity a la carte. Of course, there is an element of that in chevruta learning, but it is only an element. To be in chevruta is to look up from our own navels into the face of another human being. Chevruta is a system that necessitates social responsibility. A posture towards our neighbor that says *we are in this together.*

Chevruta also feeds the soul. Every day we read headlines about how lonely Americans are—how isolated we feel. In my personal experience, chevruta learning is an antidote to loneliness. It asks us to go deep with one person. A truly present partner. Turn off your phone. Say a blessing for the luxury of potluck learning and slow-cook friendship.

MAKE FOR YOURSELF A TEACHER

Make for yourself a teacher. — Pirkei Avot 1:6

When I was in elementary school, the week before classes began in the fall, the class lists would be posted on the front door of the school. Literally posted, like, on a printed piece of paper, taped to the glass of a physical door attached to an actual building. My friends and I would run to go see what classes we were in — did we have friends with us, or mortal enemies? Maybe most importantly, who was our teacher? What did we know about this teacher? Was she the same one my sister had? Would he be strict or a pushover? Would this new authority figure in our lives give a lot of homework or none at all? It was like a sentence being handed down from heaven. *Thus says the Lord! This will be thy teacher!*

As I got older, while there were definitely some situations where I could not avoid a certain instructor even if I tried (maybe the class was required or she was the only one who taught Chaucer), I became more and more in control of choosing the person from whom I learned. There were even some teachers who, I assume, wished that I hadn't had so much autonomy, as I have definitely been known to be a groupie for a select few intellectuals in undergrad, graduate school, and beyond (looking at you, Professors Huehls).

But *make* for yourself a teacher? Some translations instead use the word appoint, but if we are getting literal, make is a closer and more interesting translation. How do you make a teacher for yourself?

Maybe this text means we ought to turn others into teachers by changing how we see them. Ben Zoma says something to this effect later on in Pirkei Avot: *Who is wise? One who learns from all people.*[78]

But Joshua ben Perahiah doesn't say that. He says, specifically, *a teacher.* A rav. A rabbi. One.

Wait a minute. Don't rabbinical schools make rabbis? See, this was written around 200 CE, well before the rabbinical schools of today were even a twinkle in our eyes. For Joshua ben Perahiah, it is the readers, perhaps the students, who make for themselves the teachers, and not the other way around. How could this be? (And how might we take wisdom from a more emergent model? By that I mean, can someone really be taught to be a rabbi, or does a rabbi emerge from within a community? Another essay or book for another day. Turn it, turn it.)

One might argue that a teacher is not really a teacher without students. Sort of but not really like the tree falling in the woods with no one to hear it. When Joshua ben Perahiah says *Make for yourself a teacher,* he might actually mean, *Make yourself into a student.*

Yet he doesn't say that. He says, *Make for yourself a teacher.*

I'm less concerned with the particularity of the final making of the teacher and more with the action this lesson requires. The student, unlike my elementary-school self, is told not to wait for a teacher to come along. The student is told to take the reins of their own learning. It is not the teacher who needs to say, *Come learn from me.* It is the student who ought to say, *Please teach me.*

To be in the orbit of a teacher who truly delights in helping you grow is one of the greatest blessings a lifetime can afford. In our hyper-sexualized and yet repressed American society we assume the most intimate of relationships are those that include sexual intimacy without considering how other relationships can be just as intimate (if not more so) in different ways. We privilege the nuclear family and how we can stack those families in the suburbs like little boxes in a warehouse. It is so easy to assume people are only friends with people their same age and to qualify or rationalize friendships if they are more than a generation apart. I will jump on my soapbox and say that we, as an American society, do not understand the extreme importance of a teacher. We certainly don't know how to financially compensate teachers. The truth is that the value of a teacher is infinite in the seeds she sows.

Okay, there is something I'm not telling you. Joshua ben Perahiah continues in his wisdom. He starts by saying, *Make for yourself a teacher* but then immediately after he says, *Acquire for yourself a friend.*

Teachers and friends. And notice that 'teachers' comes first. In an environment of great learning, like that of the Rabbis, the teacher-student relationship was primary in one's life. Finding a teacher is like finding a partner — studying together can feel like going on a date. The anticipation before, the butterflies of excitement, the inspiration. If you know what I'm talking about you might even be nodding right now as you read.

Make for yourself a teacher is similar to how we say, *Make for yourself a friend.* We send our children to summer camp saying, *Make a friend!* but why not also encourage them to *make for yourself a teacher?* How would our world shift if we truly understood and honored this relationship? The challenge and commitment and love of this relationship. The joy of this relationship!

If you have never made a teacher for yourself, I recommend it. I recommend it in the same way I recommend choosing to forgive or to sit outside in the sun just to do so.

STUDENTS

Much Torah have I learned from my teachers, and from my colleagues more than from them, and from my students more than from all of them. — Rabbi Yehuda haNasi, Talmud Makkot 10a

Students are to Torah as wetness is to water. Anyone who has come into contact with Torah has been transformed into a student, even if just for a moment. Even teachers are transformed into students — nay, especially teachers. Arguably, teaching our children is the primary commandment concerning Torah:

These words that I am commanding you today are to be upon your hearts. And you shall teach them diligently to your children and speak of them when you sit at home and when you walk along the road, when you lie down and when you get up.[79]

These words are so central to Jewish tradition that they are part of the prayer (the Shema) we put in the mezuzot we hang in our doorways. *Always* remember to teach Torah. Whether you are home or on vacation, teach, teach, teach your children! Of course, children doesn't only mean young people. We are all children of the Jewish people as well as of our actual parents no matter how old we have grown. And even if we become the wisest elder in the village with the most incredible library of leather-bound books and an adage or story for every occasion, even then we are still students. In his book, *With Heart in Mind: Mussar Teachings to Transform Your Life*, Alan Morinis writes that a learned person is simply referred to as a great student:

The Jewish term for a learned person is not a chacham, a wise one, but a talmid chacham, which literally translates to 'a wise student.' The truly wise individual is not one who has achieved wisdom but rather one who is constantly seeking learning, ever studying more.[80]

When it comes to Torah, *all* people are students, *all* the time. However, there is also a specific category of people who are more precisely students in a given classroom or tutoring context, in relation to a specific teacher. Jewish tradition has a lot to say about how to treat these kinds of students, but perhaps the best verse to start with is one of the simplest from Pirkei Avot:

Rabbi Elazar ben Shammua said: Let the honor of your student be as dear to you as your own honor.[81]

Let's start with the possessive statement, "your student." There is something so transcendent about gathering students and knowing they are yours. There's love there — and a huge responsibility. My students. I catch myself saying "my students" a lot. Maybe this is just a proxy for my parental instincts kicking into gear. When my students walk into class (or run, as the kindergarteners do, or drag themselves pathetically, as the teens do), I always ask how they are doing — did they sleep enough last night? Why not? What's Minecraft® again? I don't know what it is but there is no sight I love more than some mildly grumpy middle schoolers sitting in a circle, convinced they are going to have the worst hour of their life as we study Torah. There is so much potential! Nowhere to go but up! They are all mine!

And what is the honor of a student? We might translate this as integrity or respect. All students are to be treated with respect — as are teachers (which includes self-respect). Their learning boundaries should be challenged for the sake of their growth, but not broken against their will. Students are not widgets you program with new, interesting information. They are organic beings that are learning about themselves as they assimilate new information and hone skills. They are discovering their own needs and preferences and figuring out how to implement or advocate for themselves. Also, they are constantly negotiating the social dimension of being in a class — who among their peers isn't paying attention to them? Who will hang out with them at the next break? If they say the thing they're thinking, will it sound weird or cool or smart or dumb? Honoring our students means honoring them as fully alive and wonderfully singular people. As our tradition teaches:

The House of Hillel says, "Every person recites [the Shema] according to their way." [82]

According to their way. Students are learning not just how to recite the Shema, but how they recite the Shema. This is like the ancient version of what we might call intelligence types or even IEPs. Even when we teach classrooms of students at a time, each individual is an entire world unto themselves! We honor our students when we honor this ahead of time and plan on the fact that our students are uniquely molded from the dust of this earth, not uniformly mass-produced like Pringles.® Students are not Pringles.®

✳✳✳

There is a great story told in the Talmud about the power of opening doors to students. Here is a streamlined version of that text:

On that day that they removed Rabban Gamliel from his position and appointed Rabbi Elazar ben Azarya in his place, there was also a fundamental change in the general approach of the study hall as they dismissed the guard at the door and permission was granted to the students to enter. Instead of Rabban Gamliel's selective approach that asserted that the students must be screened before accepting them into the study hall, the new approach asserted that anyone who seeks to study should be given the opportunity to do so.

On that day several benches were added to the study hall to accommodate the numerous students. Rabbi Yohanan said: Abba Yosef ben Dostai and the Rabbis disputed this matter. One said: Four hundred benches were added to the study hall. And one said: Seven hundred benches were added to the study hall. When he saw the tremendous growth in the number of students, Rabban Gamliel was disheartened.

There is a tradition that tractate Eduyyot was taught that day. And everywhere in the Mishna or in a baraita that they say: On that day, it is referring to that day. There was no halakha whose ruling was pending in the study hall that they did not explain and arrive at a practical halakhic conclusion. And even Rabban Gamliel did not avoid the study hall for even one moment, as he held no grudge against those who removed him from office and he participated in the halakhic discourse in the study hall as one of the Sages.[83]

Only after welcoming in more students were the most difficult legal problems solved.

✳✳✳

At the risk of ending on a nauseatingly wholesome note, the truth is that I am incredibly indebted to my students. When I teach them Torah, I learn Torah — a symbiotic relationship. My students challenge me to really know what I'm talking about, and also to humbly declare when I have no idea what I'm talking about (which is fairly often). They are my fact-checkers, editors, critics, and collaborators all rolled into one. My students force me to constantly ask and answer, *Why does this matter?* or *What does it mean to be a Jew?*

If you are or were a student of mine and reading this, thank you (Yes, even you!). May you one day be blessed with students of your own. Students who test you in your beliefs, stretch you in logical reasoning, and hold you to high standards of justice. Students who, as soon as you are getting into the depth of a discussion on a topic of grave significance, raise their hand and say with utter nonchalance, *When is this class over?*

PEOPLE OF THE BOOK

As a committed Jew, I come to ancient canonical stories, biblical, midrashic, or aggadic, with an assumption that I belong to them and they belong to me. — Rabbi Rachel Adler [84]

TaNaKh has become the Jew's companion. — Leo Trepp [85]

What is a friend? Someone you can go to when you need advice or a listening heart. Someone you can play with. A good friend challenges you when you need it and is familiar and warm and loving when you need that, too. Maybe most importantly, a friend shows up for you.

I consider the stories of the Torah to be my friends — including the genealogies and lists of laws and poems, which are all just stories in other forms. Some of these stories are old friends and some are new. Many I talk to often and others I've met in passing and haven't really hung out with in any substantial way — every year we just wave at each other from across the page. There are a few that I really look up to and plenty I wish I could change, but we all know how that goes.

I'll give you an example. The Tower of Babel is a story I've known for many years. I kind of knew it growing up — like a kid in your math class who you recognize and kind of know about because your sister and their brother used to be in the same third-grade class maybe. Like that. Anyway, around my early twenties, The Tower of Babel and I finally got some one-on-one time and a chance to bond via a Hebrew

Bible class I was taking while enrolled in divinity school. I soon came to appreciate this story as one of my favorites. It's short, easy to understand, and packs a metaphorical punch. It's straightforward upon first reading but expands the more you get to know it. I can always rely on this story when I'm in a bind for something to teach and it's a fabulous introductory text when teaching kids how to make meaning out of ancient words. Here it is so it can speak for itself:

Now the whole world had one language and a common speech. As people moved eastward, they found a plain in Shinar and settled there. They said to each other, "Come, let's make bricks and bake them thoroughly." They used brick instead of stone, and tar for mortar. Then they said, "Come, let us build ourselves a city, with a tower that reaches to the heavens, so that we may make a name for ourselves; otherwise we will be scattered over the face of the whole earth." But God came down to see the city and the tower the people were building. God said, "If as one people speaking the same language they have begun to do this, then nothing they plan to do will be impossible for them. Come, let us go down and confuse their language so they will not understand each other." So God scattered them from there over all the earth, and they stopped building the city. That is why it was called Babel — because there God confused the language of the whole world. From there God scattered them over the face of the whole earth. [86]

While this narrative is lodged in my heart as being about the awesome power of human collaboration and the primordial oneness of all people, I understand that the Tower of Babel can be read in other ways. I understand that it is multi-dimensional and accept its hope and cynicism alike.

Whenever I assign this text to students and they give their interpretations, I feel protective of the story. I really want the students and the story to get along. At the same time, my goal is for them to form their own relationship with the text, not just imitate mine.

One time a student interpreted the original builders at Babel to be like the billionaires of Silicon Valley today—power-hungry capitalists who exploit their workers. The class cheered—probably half for the capitalists and half for the student who was critiquing them. One time, a student asked about the people who didn't want to build the tower. Did they have any say in the matter? What happened to them? Were they protesting in the street like at the Women's March, she asked?

Of course I appreciated their thoughts and was impressed with their ability to connect this section of pre-Abrahamic Torah to 21st-century California. Still, I couldn't help but hear my inner voice shout, *Don't talk about my friend that way!* And if I had a dollar for every time a student told me the lesson of the story was not to upset God... let's just say I'd have a lot of dollars. It's like my students were only interested in small talk with this new friend. *How's the weather?*

I want them to understand that the story, like any one of us, is more than it first appears. First impressions can be deceiving. I want readers to choose to suspend judgment before really getting to know the text. Give the story the benefit of the doubt. Assume positive intent. I want them to hang out with the story next year (when it is read again), say hello, and ask how it's been. Because then, of course, it will ask them right back. Just as our best friends can help us learn more about ourselves, so can we chart our growth or map our current state of mind by how we interact with these stories. Stories are the best listeners.

A quick anecdote. My dear friend (a human person, not a story) was supposed to teach a lesson for a class I was a part of. Sadly, something came up and she was unable to do so. She had even prepared the text we were going to learn. It was printed and ready to go. I was asked by the organizer if I might step in in her absence, and of course I was willing. But when I asked what texts she had chosen, I was surprised at just how pleasant this substituting would be. It seems that she, too, had a particular bond with the Tower of Babel.

In a time when the Jewish people seem so fractured that we wonder if anything is holding us together at all, Torah sticks out as the obvious answer. Torah is like the mutual friend of all of the Jewish people — all Jews have an undeniable relationship to this text whether they know it or not. Whether they care or not. We differ in Shabbat observance, daily dress, family structure, dietary practice, and cholent recipes. But we all read the exact same Book.[87] We are all invited to its birthday party.

Perhaps this is what we mean when we say Jews are the People of the Book. Yes, the Torah is the book of a people — of our mythological origins, royal history, and deep wisdom. And also, we revolve around this text — orbit it. It is our hub. We are the spokes.

WHEN TORAH FEELS LIKE A BULLY

Sometimes the words of the Torah can feel like bullies. They can be harsh, unfair, or downright wicked. There is no doubt that people over the millenia have used sacred texts to intimidate and murder and enslave and oppress others in horrific ways. It behooves us to remember, however, that the Torah is the first word, not the last. It is the people who use the text for good or evil, and not necessarily the text itself. In fact, according to the Rabbis, the text is so malleable and the mind so capable, that the smartest scholars can interpret the Torah into its opposite. They write as follows:

They only place on the High Court [a person] who knows how to [interpret the laws pertaining to] a carcass of a creeping animal [which is obviously not pure to actually be] pure by Torah law. The judges on the High Court must be so skilled at logical reasoning that they could even produce a convincing argument that creeping animals, which the Torah states explicitly are ritually impure, are actually pure.[88]

For the Rabbis, the text is of course holy, but its meaning can remain unclear without thoughtful interpretation. The Torah for them is the wool from which we weave our tradition. The words have their own integrity, but no verse — no syllable! — exists without interpretation. And they do interpret the Torah into disagreeing with itself in ways that fit their moral imagination. For example, here is a very difficult and infamous text from the Torah about executing defiant children.

If a householder has a wayward and defiant son who does not heed his father or mother and does not obey them even after they discipline him, his father and mother shall take hold of him and bring him out to the elders of his town at the public meeting-place of his community. They shall say to the elders of his town, "This son of ours is disloyal and defiant; he does not heed us. He is a glutton and a drunkard." Thereupon his town's council shall stone him to death. Thus you will sweep out evil from your midst: all Israel will hear and be afraid.[89]

And here are the Rabbis arguing that the situation of this wayward child has to be so particular that it will never happen at all.

The Gemara comments: This is also taught in a baraita: Rabbi Yehuda says: If his mother was not identical to his father in voice, appearance, and height, he cannot be convicted as a stubborn and rebellious son. The Gemara asks: What is the reason for this? As the verse states: "He will not obey our voices [kolenu]" (Deuteronomy 21:20), which indicates that they both have the same voice. And since we require that they be identical in voice, we also require that they be identical in appearance and height. The Gemara asks: In accordance with whose opinion is that which is taught in a baraita*: There has never been anyone convicted as a stubborn and rebellious son and there will never be one in the future, as it is impossible to fulfill all the requirements that must be met in order to apply this halakha. And why, then, was the passage relating to a stubborn and rebellious son written in the Torah? So that you may expound upon new understandings of the Torah and receive reward for your learning, this being an aspect of the Torah that has only theoretical value.*[90]

They interpret the text out of practice. That is some fancy footwork.

But the last line is the one that gets me. According to the Rabbis, there are some verses of the Torah that only have theoretical value. That is, there are some verses that exist as thought experiments. Questions on which to chew. Which verses? How do we determine which verses are purely theoretical? Who decides?

In their essay on parashat Ki Teitzei in *Torah Queeries*, queer and trans leaders, Rabbis Elliot Kukla and Reuben Zellman attest:

Jewish tradition recognized that stoning children is an unacceptable solution to a common problem. Indeed, commentators read and reread this Torah portion to find a different, more compassionate way to understand this troubling passage. Our Sages refused to understand the verse literally.[91]

Refused to understand the verse literally implies that it was the Rabbis themselves, not some greater scheme of logic or applied exegetical method that found this law null and void. The Rabbis refused to let the text bully their community and moral sensibility. Through interpretive hoop-jumping, they forced this text to play nice.

But wait. The plot thickens! When a law can't be interpreted away, sometimes it is overturned or sidestepped in other ways. I'm talking about something called prozbul.

The Talmud teaches that one day, Hillel the Elder noticed that people were not lending money to one another because, according to Jewish law, all private loans are forgiven every seventh year, and apparently, the wealthy were hardening their hearts to those in need.[92] The Torah specifically tells us to lend money readily even though the loan might be forgiven:

Beware lest you harbor the base thought, "The seventh year, the year of loan-remission, is approaching," so that you are cruel to your needy kinsman and give him nothing.[93]

And yet, people were not lending!

So, what does Hillel do? He creates something brand new called a prozbul: a mechanism by which private loans can be transferred to a public authority and thus will not be forgiven. This way, lenders can get their money back and are more likely to give loans. This was important because people needed loans and the laws weren't working. Instead of reprimanding the community and holding the ancient text up as the final word, Hillel found a solution that actually solved the problem. In fact, his innovation was so great, our tradition teaches that it was for the betterment of the world—tikkun olam.[94]

In his book on Hillel, Rabbi Joseph Telushkin, prolific writer and democratizing teacher, writes on this great sage's motivations behind his prozbul innovation:

Hillel understood that if Judaism defined itself exclusively by literal observance of Torah law, it would end up, for example, with poor people unable to secure loans, even though securing loans was exactly what the Torah wanted to see happen. The law itself, he understood, requires a principle of tikkun olam, a standard that can be used to moderate and modify the law when it is not achieving the goal it was intended to achieve.[95]

In other words, Torah is a method through which we achieve tikkun olam—repairing the world. Or rather, Torah, in its deepest sense, teaches tikkun olam, and sometimes the laws we derive from the text ought to be drastically reinterpreted or even rewritten to realize that core teaching. And, the literal meaning of the text is not necessarily superior to the ultimate purpose of the text. One of the great Jewish thought leaders of the last century, Rabbi Mordecai Kaplan, uses the language of evolution. Sometimes we outgrow interpretations, or even beliefs.

What we so affirm may be the very antithesis of what the Torah teaches, yet since we are impelled to do so by the very aim of the Torah as a whole, we are merely extending its scope as did the Tannaim and Amoraim of old. This is simply another case of the principle that the law is sometimes fulfilled through the very suspension of it (bittulah shel Torah zehu yissudah). The text may state laws and beliefs which we have long outgrown.[96]

This is not a Torah of absolutes, but a dynamic and living Torah. A human Torah.

When the tablets were given at Mt. Sinai/Horeb from God to Moses, they were almost immediately broken. Moses comes down the mountain holding them, prepared to share the word of God with the people, and what are the people doing? They are parading around, worshiping a golden calf of their own making. Idolatry in its most literal form (Come on, guys!). Furious, Moses smashes the tablets on the ground. He goes back up the mountain and God essentially says, *It's OK, you can write a second set to replace the first pair.* Moses does. And we learn that the broken as well as the whole tablets are placed into the ark and schlepped around through the desert. The Talmud offers us a few beautiful teachings from this story. Reish Lakish teaches:

Sometimes the apparent nullification of the Torah is its foundation. As it is written: [And the Lord said to Moses: Hew for yourself two tablets of stone like the first, and I will write upon the tablets the words that were on the first tablets] which you broke (Exod. 34:1). The blessed Holy One said to Moses: Your strength was properly used in that you broke them![97]

When Torah feels like a bully, do not run from it. Face it. Face it with the tools our ancestors used: creative fortitude and patience. You might be uncomfortable. But you stand in damn good company.

Even Moses broke the laws.

TORAH IS A DOCUMENT

EZRA'S SCROLL

However the Torah came to be, it is thought to have been finished by the time Ezra came along. Ezra was a scribe and a priest—a descendant from Aaron himself—and is understood to have been born in the year 480 BCE in Babylon—in exile. He was part of the generation that, under the command of the Persian empire, was given the chance to go back and rebuild Jerusalem. While many, many Israelites opted to remain in Babylon, Ezra decides to return toting some very important luggage.

Ezra came up from Babylon, a scribe expert in the [Torah] of Moses.[98]

Up until he arrives in Jerusalem, there is no record of the Torah of Moses.[99] Some scholars even consider Ezra to have been the final compiler of the texts that make up the Torah. In other words, when we look at the question of who wrote the Torah from a historical-critical perspective, many theories entertain the idea that Torah is a compilation of different sources woven together over time into what we today call The Torah. We will get more into this in the coming chapters. For now, suffice it to say that there are scholars who consider Ezra to have been alive right around the time that this was happening. In *Introduction to the Hebrew Bible*, biblical scholar John J. Collins writes:

In Jewish tradition Ezra is revered as the person who restored the law of Moses, and it is generally assumed that his law was the Torah as we have it. Some modern scholars also credit Ezra with the final edition of the Pentateuch, incorporating the Priestly strand.[100]

In his historical account, *From the Maccabees to the Mishnah*, Shaye J.D. Cohen writes:

During the Persion period, a book emerged that was known as 'the Torah of Moses.' It was the product of centuries of tradition, both written and oral, but now its various strands (J, E, P, H, D, and others) were intertwined for the final time, and editorial activity ceased.[101]

Either Ezra was in the room where it happened or at least knew a guy who knew a guy who was there. He was not just a scribe but an expert—the prototypical Torah scholar and teacher.[102] Regardless of whether Ezra was the compiler, he is credited as the first to *share* the Torah with the people of Jerusalem. The following is a slightly redacted account of what we get from the Book of Nehemiah:

The entire people assembled as one man in the square before the Water Gate, and they asked Ezra the scribe to bring the scroll of the Teaching of Moses with which God had charged Israel. On the first day of the seventh month, Ezra the priest brought the Teaching before the congregation, men and women and all who could listen with understanding. He read from it, facing the square before the Water Gate, from the first light until midday, to the men and the women and those who could understand; the ears of all the people were included toward the scroll of the Teaching...

Ezra opened the scroll in the sight of all the people, for he was above all the people; as he opened it, all the people stood up. Ezra blessed God, and all the people answered, "Amen, Amen," with hands upraised. Then they bowed their heads and prostrated themselves before God with their faces to the ground. Jeshua, Bani, Sherebiah, Jamin, Akkub, Shabbethai, Hodiah, Maaseiah, Kelita, Azariah, Jozabad, Hanan, Pelaiah, and the Levites explained the Teaching to the people, while the people stood in their places. They read from the scroll of the Teaching of God, translating it and giving the sense; so they understood the reading...

On the second day, the heads of the clans of all the people and the priests and Levites gathered to Ezra the scribe to study the words of the Teaching.[103]

From its first public reading, the Torah had to be explained. Either its plain sense wasn't clear, the people didn't speak Hebrew, or for some other reason. It was translated, taught, and interpreted that very day in the town square. Men and women were both listening. There were blessings. The people saw the scroll. It was theirs.

Cohen accounts that Ezra's public reading was a political as much as a spiritual act.

Ezra read to the public 'the book of the instruction [Torah] of Moses' and, assisted by the Levites, explained its meaning (Neh. 8). Deut. 31:10–13 had commanded the assembled Israelites to hear 'the Torah' read aloud every seventh year; Ezra took this idea and ran with it, not only reading the Torah but also explaining it. In effect, Ezra "published" the Torah by making it accessible to the masses. This was a direct threat to the political hegemony of the priesthood... By giving the masses free access to the Torah, Ezra was curbing the power of the priestly magistrates.[104]

By reading the Torah aloud, and making clear it was a particular and discrete thing, the power was transferred from the priests themselves to the text. Whereas few people will ever become priests, all people can learn Torah.

The story of Ezra is essential to how we understand Torah study today. In my experience, there is an assumption that some people have about Torah study that in the good old days, everyone could partake in it seamlessly and naturally. That everyone knew Hebrew or was equally knowledgeable on matters of the text. But it is not so. The story of Ezra teaches us that, from the get-go, Torah needed to be explained. Teachers were essential. Today's struggles with learning Torah do not represent a failure to live up to the standard from some golden age. In some ways, today's struggles with learning Torah are the most authentic expression of what was happening during the first moment the Torah was read to the people.

LIKE US, FULL OF CONTRADICTIONS

To approach texts critically is not to dismiss them. On the contrary, it can be part of what it means to take sources seriously as a modern person. When we understand the meaning of a religious text in and for its time, we are freer to take the text and apply it to our own time.

— Judith Plaskow [105]

I've been trying to write this for some time — maybe even since high school. In high school, I read *Who Wrote The Bible?* by Richard Elliott Friedman and felt closer to Jewish wisdom than ever before. See, I've never believed the Torah dropped from heaven into Moses' hands. I believe it is a sacred text, but what that means has always been a matter of changing interpretation.

Marrying historical approaches to the Torah with more traditional takes on the text was one of the reasons I applied to graduate school in the first place. How can historical criticism and archeology reinvigorate Torah study? How can science enliven narrative and awaken the spirit?

Specifically, and as alluded to in the previous chapter, I am talking about Documentary Hypothesis.[106] Documentary Hypothesis is just that, a possible answer to the question of who wrote the Hebrew Bible. By the mid-17th century, there were some sizable doubts surrounding

Mosaic authorship. In fact, according to Joel Baden, professor of Hebrew Bible at Yale University (and a teacher of mine. Hi Joel! He told me to call him Joel), the text itself does not claim Moses as its author:

The Pentateuch itself makes no claim for Mosaic authorship; the tradition that Moses wrote the five books was both an unintentional by-product of inner-biblical developments and an intentionally articulated article of faith for both Jewish and Christian religious groups.[107]

But if Moses didn't write the Torah, who did?

This is very roughly what the Documentary Hypothesis says: the Torah is a compilation of documents from four different sources (and maybe five if you count the compilers). The sources tell different versions of key stories, have different names for places and people, different names for God, and different priorities. They even have different writing styles. Over some period of time, these documents were pieced together into what we call the Torah (Five Books of Moses, Pentateuch, etc.). So, Mosaic authorship, but in another way.

Here's the thing: the compilers preserved the different versions and names and places in the very structure of the text. So much so, that even the first story of the entire Torah, creation, includes two vastly different versions. You can read them both here:

CREATION 1: GENESIS 1:1–2:3

In the beginning when God created the heavens and the earth, the earth was a formless void and darkness covered the face of the deep, while a wind from God swept over the face of the waters. Then God said, "Let there be light;" and there was light. And God saw that the light was good; and God separated the light from the darkness. God called the light Day, and the darkness God called Night. And there was evening and there was morning, the first day.

And God said, "Let there be a dome in the midst of the waters, and let it separate the waters from the waters." So God made the dome and separated the waters that were under the dome from the waters that were above the dome. And it was so. God called the dome Sky. And there was evening and there was morning, the second day.

And God said, "Let the waters under the sky be gathered together into one place, and let the dry land appear." And it was so. God called the dry land Earth, and the waters that were gathered together he called seas. And God saw that it was good. Then God said, "Let the earth put forth vegetation: plants yielding seed, and fruit trees of every kind on earth that bear fruit with the seed in it." And it was so. The Earth brought forth vegetation: plants yielding seed of every kind, and trees of every kind bearing fruit with the seed in it. And God saw that it was good. And there was evening and there was morning, the third day.

And God said, "Let there be lights in the dome of the sky to separate the day from the night; and let them be for signs and for seasons and for days and years, and let them be lights in the dome of the sky to give light upon the earth." And it was so. God made the two great lights—the greater light to rule the day and the lesser light to rule the night—and the stars. God set them in the dome of the sky to give light upon the Earth, to rule over the day and over the night, and to separate the light from the darkness. And God saw that it was good. And there was evening and there was morning, the fourth day.

And God said, "Let the waters bring forth swarms of living creatures, and let birds fly above the earth across the dome of the sky." So God created the great sea monsters and every living creature that moves, of every kind, with which the waters swarm, and every winged bird of every kind. And God saw that it was good. God blessed them, saying, "Be fruitful and multiply and fill the waters in the seas, and let birds *multiply on the earth." And there was evening and there was morning, the fifth day.*

And God said, "Let the earth bring forth living creatures of every kind: cattle and creeping things and wild animals of the earth of every kind." And it was so. God made the wild animals of the earth of every kind, and the cattle of every kind, and everything that creeps upon the ground of every kind. And God saw that it was good. Then God said, "Let us make humankind in our image, according to our likeness; and let them have dominion over the fish of the sea, and over the birds of the air, and over the cattle, and over all the wild animals of the earth, and over every creeping thing that creeps upon the earth." So God created humankind in God's image, in the image of God God created them; male and female God created them.

God blessed them, and God said to them, "Be fruitful and multiply, and fill the earth and subdue it; and have dominion over the fish of the sea and over the birds of the air and over every living thing that moves upon the earth." God said, "See, I have given you every plant yielding seed that is upon the face of all the earth, and every tree with seed in its fruit; you shall have them for food. And to every beast of the earth, and to every bird of the air, and to everything that creeps on the earth, everything that has the breath of life, I have given every green plant for food." And it was so. God saw everything that God had made, and indeed, it was very good. And there was evening and there was morning, the sixth day.

Thus the heavens and the Earth were finished, and all their multitude. And on the seventh day God finished the work that God had done, and God rested on the seventh day from all the work that God had done. So God blessed the seventh day and hallowed it, because on it God rested from all the work that God had done in creation.

CREATION 2: GENESIS 2:4–25

In the day that God made the Earth and the heavens, when no plant of the field was yet in the Earth and no herb of the field had yet sprung up—for God had not caused it to rain upon the Earth, and there was no one to till the ground; but a stream would rise from the Earth, and water the whole face of the ground—then God formed man from the dust of the ground, and breathed into his nostrils the breath of life; and the man became a living being. And God planted a garden in Eden, in the east; and there God put the man whom God had formed. Out of the ground God made to grow every tree that is pleasant to the sight and good for food, the tree of life also in the midst of the garden, and the tree of the knowledge of good and evil.

A river flows out of Eden to water the garden, and from there it divides and becomes four branches. The name of the first is Pishon; it is the one that flows around the whole land of Havilah, where there is gold; and the gold of that land is good; bdellium and onyx stone are there. The name of the second river is Gihon; it is the one that flows around the whole land of Cush. The name of the third river is Tigris, which flows east of Assyria. And the fourth river is the Euphrates.

God took the man and put him in the garden of Eden to till it and keep it. And God commanded the man, "You may freely eat of every tree of the garden; but of the tree of the knowledge of good and evil you shall not eat, for in the day that you eat of it you shall die."

Then God said, "It is not good that the man should be alone; I will make him a helper as his partner." So out of the ground God formed every animal of the field and every bird of the air, and brought them to the man to see what he would call them; and whatever the man called every living creature, that was its name. The man gave names to all cattle, and to the birds of the air, and to every animal of the field; but for the man there was not found a helper as his partner. So God caused a deep sleep to fall upon the man, and he slept; then God removed one of his sides and closed up its place with flesh. And the side that God had taken from the man God made into a woman and brought her to the man. Then the man said, "This at last is bone of my bones, and flesh of my flesh, this one shall be called Woman, for out of Man this one was taken."

Therefore a man leaves his father and his mother and clings to his wife, and they become one flesh. And the man and his wife were both naked, and were not ashamed.

If that was too much text for one sitting, here's a recap: in the first story, people were created last, and were created male and female at the exact same time, in God's image. In the second, Adam was created first, animals were created to keep him company (but they weren't good enough at curing his loneliness), and Eve was created from his side. Was Adam the first mother? Was Adam one being brimming with both male and female potential? The answers to those questions are another book for another time. Other differences: In the first story, there is no Garden of Eden. In the second, there is. In the first story, we get Shabbat and creation in six days. In the second story, nope. And there are many more differences (not to mention the serpent and the fruit of the Tree of Knowledge of Good and Evil, etc.).

According to Documentary Hypothesis, the reason for these two versions is simple—they are just two versions of a creation myth, from different groups of people under the Israelite umbrella—maybe from different times throughout the development of peoples and their cultures. The more interesting thing is that they are both preserved, one after another, at the beginning of the Torah. The compiler didn't choose which was better but instead united them, like an anthology.

A more traditional Jewish approach interprets this as different—or even contradictory—perspectives of the same event. A historical approach simply notices how interesting it is that both stories exist.

What can this tell us about the culture of the time, how the compilers understood their job, and what the goal of the Torah was?

Let's get back to considering the different sources. Here are a few more concrete examples of different versions of the same thing:

Moses' fathers-in-law is called Reuel in Exodus 2:18 and Jethro in Exodus 3:1. (Is it possible that Moses had two father-in-laws either because he had multiple wives or because his father-in-law was married to another man?! Yes, but unlikely.) There are two versions of Jacob being renamed Israel: Genesis 32:29 and Genesis 35:10. Aaron seems to die in two different places: Mount Hor in Numbers 20:23–29 and Moserah in Deuteronomy 10:6. Look them up and see!

The point of this essay is not to convince you of Documentary Hypothesis, or even to teach it to you in full. If you want to learn more about it, I highly recommend Professor Joel Baden's book, *The Composition of the Pentateuch: Renewing the Documentary Hypothesis*. And, to keep it nice and balanced, there are plenty of criticisms of this hypothesis out there that you can find. I encourage you to investigate for yourself.

The point of this chapter is to claim the following: the Torah was born, already in conversation with itself. It was born, already unresolved in how to tell the story. Or rather, it was born with an understanding that *the story* is not limited to one version. The Torah, even when bound and held up as one object, is radically discordant.

Let's go a little bit further. As I argue in the next chapter, the different sources also had different motivations or goals. For example, the source called the Priestly source, or "P" for short, is very concerned with the laws of the priests (and is a bit more monotone than the other sources, if I do say so myself). The source which we call the Elohist source, or "E," may be more interested in the role of dreams than the other sources. Now, sure, we can't know exactly what happened with the compilers when these texts were put together around the 400s BCE. But I'd like to think that their personalities, anxieties, and priorities were preserved. Not unlike today's global Jewish community: our priorities, anxieties, and personalities differ, too. Even contradict. Even drastically, sometimes.

In the Torah's composition we find a reflection of Jewish life. Discord and contradiction. It is almost as if it is in our DNA to be a *compiled people*. Not only the Torah but *we* were never cut from one cloth.

So, how can this inform our study today? What if, when reading parashat hashavuah (the weekly Torah portion) we reached for historical criticism as well as Rashi? Or maybe we can find meaning in the overlap of priorities — on what do the sources agree? Might there be extra importance to be found there? To me, bringing Torah study into the 21st century means also embracing a historical approach.

The rest of this book is a testament to the fact that I do not believe embracing historical criticism makes the Torah any less sacred. And I pose the following question to you: how might considering historical approaches even increase the great life-bringing power of our central words?

A NEW ARGUMENT ABOUT THOSE LINES IN LEVITICUS

What does the Torah say about gay people? That's a trick question. There is no such thing as gay people in the Torah. There are, however, two somewhat confusing verses in the Book of Leviticus that comment upon men lying with men. It is widely accepted that this means penetrative sex, and there are sources all over the place that argue why these two verses are clear or not clear or prohibit gayness or don't. But there is one argument I'm excited to share that I think will make a new kind of sense for our contemporary historically-inclined sensibilities. Here are the texts:

Do not lie with a male the lyings of a woman; it is an abhorrence.[108]

If a man lies with a male the lyings of a woman, the two of them have done an abhorrent thing; they shall be put to death — their bloodguilt is upon them.[109]

There are many excellent arguments and interpretations of these texts (and others) that champion a fully integrated and realized Jewish and gay life. An excellent place to start is with Rabbi Steven Greenberg's *Wrestling With God & Men: Homosexuality in the Jewish Tradition.* And additional scholars on whose shoulders I stand are Judith Plaskow, Rabbi

Elliot Kukla, Maggid Jhos Singer, Joshua Lesser, Gregg Drinkwater, David Shneer, Rabbi Benay Lappe, Noam Sienna, and many, many, many more.

Here is an argument of my own I want to share. It relies on the idea that repetition signals importance — the more the Torah repeats something, the more we need to pay attention to it. For example, we are told many, many times to love the stranger as ourselves. To name a few:

You shall not wrong a stranger or oppress him.[110]

The stranger who resides with you shall be to you as one of your citizens; you shall love him as yourself, for you were strangers in the land of Egypt: I the Sovereign am your God.[111]

Love your neighbor as yourself: I am God.[112]

You too must befriend the stranger, for you were strangers in the land of Egypt.[113]

These are only seven examples of many such teachings. But men lying with men? Twice. To boot, they occur within the same source. And now, hang onto your hats while I apply the Documentary Hypothesis. But before I do, a recap: In the Documentary Hypothesis, the Torah was created by compilers (which might be a school, a line of scholars, or a few people) piecing together multiple documents from multiple sources over time. Documentary Hypothesis suggests that there were four major documents, each with different motivations, audiences, versions of stories, and even names for places and people — Mt. Sinai is also called Mt. Horeb, for example.

Within this hypothesis, we find that the lines in Leviticus about men lying with men come from the same source, which we call the Priestly source, or P, for short. P was concerned with ritual laws and genealogy, and wrote in a style that reminds me of Ikea instructions. But wait! There's more! Within the Priestly source there is a sublayer which we call the Holiness Code, or H. It is within this particular section that we find those lines. It's like Russian Doll Torah: lines within a source, within a source, within the whole.

Furthermore, there are two other places in the Torah that discuss what we call sexual morality laws: Deuteronomy 22:13–28 and Exodus 22:15–18 (which we call the Covenant Code). In both of these places, there is no mention of men lying with men or other laws against what would be understood today as gay stuff. Additionally, because the Deuteronomic source is considered to be the latest source, one might conclude that even if men lying with men was an issue for the Holiness Code source, by the time Deuteronomy rolls around, maybe it was no longer a significant concern.

This is the point: these two laws in Leviticus, which have caused so much death and suffering, were clearly only important to one of the four sources of the Torah, and further, to one subset within that one source. In other words, men lying with men doesn't seem to have been important for the other three sources, or for the compilers, who really had the last word.

Now, I hear you thinking, okay, but if I cared what the Torah said about men lying with men in the first place—if I was a more traditional Jew—then I likewise wouldn't be inclined to apply Documentary Hypothesis to the text in the first place. This is a good point. It is likely that only someone who is more experimental with how they read Torah would be willing to use this approach. And someone who is more experimental may also not worry too much about what the Torah does or does not say about men lying with men. So, allow me to just speak personally.

As a gay Jew—and one who has been raised and made her home in the most progressive place on the planet — those lines in Leviticus don't have much sway over my life. This is a testament both to the queer scholars that I mentioned above (and many more unnamed to whom I am forever indebted) and to the way I engage with the text. But, what this approach has illuminated for me is that maybe, for the other sources and the people proximate to their time and place, it didn't have much sway on their lives, either. When I apply Documentary Hypothesis to the text a possible world emerges where for many groups of early Jews, men lying with men was commonplace — maybe even taken for granted. Maybe those lines in Leviticus were actually not the norm for the time, but the oppressive outlier.

I'll repeat (in different words) what I said in the past chapter because it bears repeating. I add this argument to the conversation because I believe the way we read the Torah needs to expand to include archeological and historical criticism. For me, the Torah didn't fall from the sky. However, I do believe it is sacred and must be read with respect and curiosity, in community. When done so, the Torah offers us great wisdom. However, if we kid ourselves about why we read it, we will teach our children that our Torah and all of our rituals surrounding it are all together nothing more than nostalgic performance. Empty. To me, that is the death of Torah.

If we are honest about looking at all of the evidence concerning where the Torah came from, we actually create more opportunity for connection to it.

How beautiful that this text, in its knit-together form, preserves multiple versions. The Torah was born in disagreement, conversation, and compromise. It was born holding multiple perspectives. So, sure, maybe the Holiness Code disapproved of men lying with men. But the other sources didn't.

How can historical analysis illuminate how we read Torah as Jews today?

TAKE TWO

Many great things come in twos. Two wheels on a bicycle. Two slices of bread for a sandwich (unless it's open-faced). We brush our teeth twice a day (most of us). Two lungs. Two thumbs. Did you know there are two versions of the Ten Commandments? First, we read them when God gives them at Mt. Sinai/Horeb in the Book of Exodus. Then, again, Moses retells them in the Book of Deuteronomy as the Israelites are preparing to enter the Promised Land. They are more or less identical except for one glaring difference: the commandment regarding Shabbat. In the Exodus version, we read the following:

EXODUS 20:8–11

Remember the sabbath day and keep it holy. Six days you shall labor and do all your work, but the seventh day is a sabbath of your God: you shall not do any work — you, your son or daughter, your male or female slave, or your cattle, or the stranger who is within your settlements. For in six days יהוה made heaven and earth and sea — and all that is in them — and then rested on the seventh day; therefore יהוה blessed the sabbath day and hallowed it.

The key commandment here is to remember Shabbat. The verb is zachor, and the reasoning for the commandment is the story of creation. God rested on day seven so you will rest on day seven. But then we get something very different in Deuteronomy.

DEUTERONOMY 5:12–15

Observe the sabbath day to keep it holy, as your God, יהוה, has commanded you. Six days you shall labor and do all your work, but the seventh day is a sabbath of your God, יהוה; you shall not do any work — you, your son or your daughter, your male or female slave, your ox or your ass, or any of your cattle, or the stranger in your settlements, so that your male and female slave may rest as you do. Remember that you were a slave in the land of Egypt and your God, יהוה, freed you from there with a mighty hand and an outstretched arm; therefore your God, יהוה, has commanded you to observe the sabbath day.

Here, the key commandment is to observe or guard or keep Shabbat. The verb is shamor, and the reason for the commandment is the story of the exodus. God freed you from Egypt and so you are obligated to follow God's laws, one of which is the sabbath.

These are two completely different approaches to the same practice, so what are we supposed to do? Remember or guard? How are those things different, and how do different rituals manifest those mitzvot (commandments)? The Talmud answers this in a very Talmudic way which takes into account the all-at-onceness of Torah time. Remember, there is no timeline in Torah.

"Remember the Sabbath day, to keep it holy" (Exodus 20:8), and: "Observe the Sabbath day, to keep it holy" (Deuteronomy 5:12), were spoken in one utterance, in a manner that the human mouth cannot say and that the human ear cannot hear.[114]

Both commandments are actually one — said at once in a way Earth-bound humans cannot fully comprehend. One commandment is not primary and the other secondary. They are simultaneous. Like mixing a cocktail. Greater than the sum of their parts.

Another interpretation is that Moses remembered it wrong, or added onto it in his retelling. He wanted to share another dimension of Shabbat.

But what if we consider these differences within a historical-critical framework? Deuteronomy is its own source which represents one particular orientation towards Shabbat, while the source of the Exodus text is considered to be different from that of Deuteronomy. So let's say we have different orientations towards Shabbat that reflect different schools of thought or traditions, and thus different groups of people. Is it possible that the rationale for Shabbat was different for different groups of Judeans? It is possible!

Shabbat is not the only Jewish practice in which we find a coming-together of traditions. There is a similar combining of practices in how we blow shofar, and even the Ashkenazi tradition of hanging the mezuzah. Let's look at both of these.

In his book, *The Jewish Way: Living the Holidays*, Rabbi Irving

Greenberg teaches about the history of why we make the shofar sounds we make today.[115] The following is an adaptation of his teaching:

In the month of Tishrei, we hear the shofar—a ram's horn that is turned into an instrument like a trumpet—many, many times in a few different ways. That is, there are two primary calls of the shofar. Tekiah is a long, straight blast—nine beats long. Sages of generations past interpreted this sound to represent joy, hope and trust in the future! The second sound is called teruah. This sound is made up of three broken or wavering sounds that represent a cry for mercy or forgiveness. There were two different traditions, however, and each performed this call a little differently.

One group of people thought that teruah was a slower moaning sound, expressed in three broken sounds, each three beats long; they called this shevarim, which means broken. Another group of people thought it sounded more like a vigorous cry for help. They would sound the shofar in nine (three times three) staccato, almost bleating sounds. They named this teruah, which means alarm-sound.

After the destruction of the Temple, these two different Jewish communities found themselves in the same place and had to figure out which way to sound the shofar for the holidays. To keep the people together and help bridge the new community, the Head Rabbi decided that a set of each sound version be blown, and, for good measure, a third set incorporating both broken sounds together also be sounded. This became the tradition that is still in practice today.

Let's consider another example: the story of why Ashkenazi Jews hang the mezuzah on a slant. This explanation comes from Rabbi Ruth Adar, the *Coffee Shop Rabbi* as she is known online. She writes:

It all goes back to a family debate and technical discussion. Rashi and his grandson Rabbeinu Tam disagreed about the proper way to hang a mezuzah. Rashi believed that the mezuzah should be upright, just as the Torah scroll is upright when it is properly stored in the Ark at the synagogue. Rabbenu Tam said, no! — the mezuzah should be horizontal, just as it is when it is laid on the table to read it.

We get this story from Rabbi Jacob ben Asher, the great Jewish legal writer. He writes in the Tur, his code of Jewish Law, that "careful people" will do their best to fulfill BOTH directions by placing the mezuzah on a slant. However, while that is the custom in the Ashkenazi world, Sephardim prefer to follow the ruling of Rashi and hang their mezuzot vertically.[116]

Let's return to Shabbat. What if the existence of two approaches to Shabbat, shamor v'zachor, to guard and to remember, means that different communities had different language for, and ultimate reasons for, Shabbat? How could our understanding of Shabbat and *correct* Shabbat practice change if we consider that Shabbat was practiced in various ways from the very beginning? There is a big gap between the commandment to guard and remember. What might Shabbat practices have looked like before these were combined?

Or, what if we focus on the motivation, not the specific verbs used in the command language? That is, both say there is this thing we do called the sabbath, but for different reasons — creation or the exodus. Similarly, folks study Torah for different reasons. Some study because the text is the direct word of God. Some study because Torah is our ancestral wisdom literature. Some study because it connects them to their present community. The action is shared, but not the *why*. By combining these two Shabbat laws, we are reminded that there might be multiple reasons for a shared practice. By thinking about these two Shabbat laws as originating independently, we consider that each reason stands alone.

Let's end with a classic Jewish joke on this topic, the question of motivation.

Child: Abba, why do you go to shul?

Abba: What kind of a question is that?

Child: I know you are a non-believer, an atheist, an agnostic, or whatever. I know you aren't talking to God, so why would you go to shul?

Abba: Goldberg goes to shul.

Child: So what? What kind of an answer is that?

Abba: Goldberg goes to shul to talk to God; I go to shul to talk to Goldberg!

TORAH IS A PLAYGROUND

WHAT IS THIS STORY NOT TELLING ME?

The Rabbis could not help but believe that his wondrous and sacred text, the Torah, was intended for all Jews and for all times. Surely God could foresee the need for new interpretations; all interpretations, therefore, are already in the Torah text. — Barry W. Holtz [117]

What was the conversation at the dinner table the evening before Moses' family decided to put three-month-old Moses in the basket and send him down the Nile River? Did everyone agree this was the thing to do? Were there other ideas floated around? Did they ever consider fleeing Egypt altogether? Or what about Queen Vashti — where does she go after she famously denies King Ahashverosh's demands in the Book of Esther? Does she move away and start a feminist bookstore?

Torah has a lot of gaps. It has gaps in narrative and logic and emotion and time. You can think of these like potholes in a road. Luckily, we know how to fill a hole in a text. We fill it in with another text. Sometimes this text is borrowed from elsewhere and other times it is entirely made up. This story spackle is what we call midrash. For Barry Holtz, contributing writer and editor of *Back to the Sources: Reading The Classic Jewish Texts*, midrash means two different things:

First, midrash (deriving from the Hebrew root "to search out") is the process of interpreting. The object of interpretation is the Bible or, on occasion, other sacred texts; second, midrash refers to the corpus of work that has collected these interpretations, works such as midrash Rabbah... The great flowering of midrash was roughly between the years 400 and 1200 CE. But it is important to note that originally, midrashic literature was oral — sermons preached in the synagogues and teachings of various sages.[118]

There are tons of midrashim you might be familiar with — so familiar, in fact, you might even have thought they were actually in the Torah. Take, for example, the story of Abraham and the idols. This story was created to explain why, from all the people in the whole world, God chose Abraham. Here's the original midrash, from *Bereishit Rabbah* (Terah is Abraham's father, by the way):

Rabbi Hiyya the grandson of Rabbi Adda of Yaffo [said]: Terah was a worshiper of idols. One time he had to travel to a place, and he left [his son] Abraham in charge of his store. When a man would come in to buy [idols], Abraham would ask: How old are you? They would reply: fifty or sixty. Abraham would then respond: Woe to him who is sixty years old and worships something made today — the customer would be embarrassed, and would leave. A woman entered carrying a dish full of flour. She said to him: this is for you, offer it before them. Abraham took a club in his hands and broke all of the idols, and placed the club in the hands of the biggest idol. When his father returned, he asked: who did all of this? Abraham replied: I can't hide it from you — a woman came carrying a dish of flour and told me to offer it before them. I did, and one of them said 'I will eat it first,' and another said I will eat it first.' The biggest one rose, took a club, and smashed the rest of them. Terah said: what, do you think you can trick me? They don't have cognition! Abraham said: Do your ears hear what your mouth is saying? [119]

This story is trying to show that, because Abraham was particularly suspicious of idols and was willing to destroy them (even if they belonged to his own father) while educating people along the way, he was the right guy to be dubbed First Hebrew Patriarch. This story helps us feel an affinity towards our forefather. His wit is sharp and his principles are clear. This story gives a stronger foundation not only to God's choice in Abraham but to the entire Abrahamic covenant.

The Rabbis were able to open their minds and think creatively about the texts because, for them, the text was given by a perfect author — God — and had an infinite potential to be interpreted in new ways. They would take verses from various parts of the TaNaKh to address the problem at hand because the text was all connected — all happening at once and in conversation with itself. Additionally, the Rabbis were able to open their minds and think creatively because they *had to*. The Second Temple had fallen. Torah as they knew it was over. A new moment was being born. Time to get creative or bury Jewish life for good.

Writing midrash today (what we will be calling modern midrash) is like writing Torah fan fiction — it bridges the world and time of the text with the world and time of the reader. It keeps the text relevant in changing cultural and theological contexts. And as Judith Plaskow and many other feminist Jewish scholars teach, it can also be a method by which those on the margins can reclaim Jewish literary space.

Midrash gives a voice to those who are hidden. As Holtz writes, *Where the Bible is mysterious and silent, midrash comes to unravel the mystery.* [120]

The following sections will include new and original modern midrashim, written by me and inspired by the question: what is this story not telling me? In the tradition of Plaskow, each chapter will be about a woman in Torah who has more story to tell than the text allows. The chapters will begin with a little background on the character in question and then move into a monologue from the character's perspective. My hope is that, if we listen carefully, we can hear them.

MODERN MIDRASH: EVE'S LAUNCH

We all know the story of Eve and that fateful bite — eating the fruit of the Tree of Knowledge of Good and Evil. But in case you forgot, here is a refresher. Eve is created out of Adam's side with the expressed intention to be his companion. They are given all of the fruit in the garden to eat except for the fruit that comes from the Tree of Knowledge of Good and Evil. Enter the serpent.

Now the serpent was the shrewdest of all the wild beasts that God had made. It said to the woman, "Did God really say: You shall not eat of any tree of the garden?" The woman replied to the serpent, "We may eat of the fruit of the other trees of the garden. It is only about fruit of the tree in the middle of the garden that God said: 'You shall not eat of it or touch it, lest you die.'" And the serpent said to the woman, "You are not going to die, but God knows that as soon as you eat of it your eyes will be opened and you will be like divine beings who know good and bad." When the woman saw that the tree was good for eating and a delight to the eyes, and that the tree was desirable as a source of wisdom, she took of its fruit and ate. She also gave some to her husband, and he ate. Then the eyes of both of them were opened and they perceived that they were naked; and they sewed together fig leaves and made themselves loincloths.[121]

How would Eve tell her own story? What is this story not telling me? What follows is an original modern midrash, written by me, from Eve's perspective, attempting an answer.

✳✳✳

Yes, I ate it. And I'd do it again. What would you do if you were me?

Consider this: I was born into captivity. A garden, but a prison. Guarded by angels. Created to serve Adam, I was never granted a childhood, and my life was set out before me to be, quite frankly, boring. Stagnant. Proscribed. Can we even call Gan Eden beautiful without having ever known the alternative? It was too safe. The kind of safe that smells faintly of latex and industrial floor cleaner drying on a linoleum floor with orange cones all over the place. Hints of bleach. People talk about it like it was this great womb of lush flora and fauna but they forget it was more like Pleasantville than not. And if it was a womb, we were overdue. I couldn't live like that. Though alive, I'd argue that at that time I wasn't even truly living.

Thousands of years later, I watched as followers of Jesus Christ started calling it "The Fall" or "Original Sin." They said the serpent bamboozled me as if I was some pathetic sitting duck. I knew exactly what I was doing, and when I look back on that day, I consider it to be "The Launch."

Adam thanked me.

Do I wish I had had better PR? Sure, it would have saved us all a lot of ache and murder. But if there's one thing I've learned in all my eons, it's that people talk. You can't control it. They will call you what they want to call you. Disobedient. Wicked. Stupid. Weak-willed. They love a good scapegoat, even if it is me, the mother of all humanity. So much for honoring your parents. Let them talk. They will never know what it meant to feel the veil of Eden slip from our eyes. The numb of Eden. The dull, monotonous humming of Eden. They only wrote that I noticed I was naked and made myself some clothes. That's all they cared about anyway, my body. My body was a different kind of forbidden fruit. They didn't write that when I took that bite, suddenly, I could hear my own heartbeat like a drum calling me. When I took that bite the flavor was so rich and divinely sweet — God took on a whole new meaning.

They wrote that we were banished. I say, we finally broke free.

MODERN MIDRASH: NA'AMAH'S NIGHTMARE

Noah is a pretty popular guy. One of the most well-known figures from the Torah, he is famous for being righteous in his generation, building an ark, saving all the animals (including, unfortunately, the mosquitos), and being played by Russell Crowe and Steve Carell in major motion pictures. But you know who almost no one knows? His wife, Na'amah. Na'amah was a descendant of Cain and, let's be honest; she went through more than most people in the Torah. She was one of our primordial (though unsung) matriarchs — we all descend from her. But who was she? The Torah doesn't say much about her at all, but luckily, we find more details in midrash and medieval commentary. Here are two examples:

And the sister of Tubal-Cain was Na'amah. Rabbi Abba bar Kahana said: Na'amah was Noah's wife. Why was she called Na'amah? Because all of her deeds were pleasant (ne'imim). The Rabbis said this referred to a different Na'amah. Why was this woman called Na'amah? Because she beat on a drum to draw people to idol worship.[122]

In Bereishit Rabbah (23:3) they say that she was the wife of Noah, and why was she called Na'ama? For her deeds were pleasant and pleasing. What they intended was that she was known in those generations for she was a righteous woman and gave birth to righteous ones, and thus the text mentions her. If this is so, then a remnant of Cain remains in the world, and if you say that this is not the wife that Noah had three children with, then why is she mentioned?[123]

So much is missing from her story and I am left with many, many questions.

Namely, when Noah came home the night after God first talked to him, what happened? How did he tell Na'amah? How did she respond? What is this story not telling me? What follows is an original modern midrash, written by me, from Na'amah's perspective, attempting to answer these questions.

***

I will never forget the night he came home because he had tears in his eyes. Noah never cried. Not when our boys were born. Not when his father died. Not even when his beloved mother died in his arms. But he had tears in his eyes and it frightened me.

We were silent for a while. Hours. Cleaning up after our days. We ate in silence. The sounds of our chewing and slurping felt amplified and ominous next to our conspicuous quiet. I knew he'd tell me when he was ready, and meanwhile, the air between us was thick like molasses and buzzing like lightning. A heavy energy.

Finally, as we were lying in bed he told me something I could barely believe. He said a voice spoke to him — a cold voice that boomed as if the clouds themselves were the speakers. Drums.

"I am about to destroy them with the Earth."

I wanted to stop him and say he must have dozed off or hadn't had enough to eat or — he started shaking. He knows what he heard, he said. He said this voice told him a flood was coming and it would kill everything. He was to build a boat. Everything would die — drown — but us. The world was starting over.

Almost everything in me would have screamed a million times that there was some rational explanation for this and he should just rest his eyes now and go to sleep. But I didn't. There was something in the register of his voice. It was real. He was crying again — big full tears like raindrops.

I held him close, rocking him like I used to rock the boys after they'd woken in the night with bad dreams. We rocked back and forth for some time — a strange foreshadowing I would soon learn during our long nights on board. I held him every night then too. His tears didn't stop until his last day.

But that night he fell asleep first. And then I did, some hours later. This was my dream.

I dreamed we would build this boat and millions would die and we would have no choice but to begin again. I dreamed God said it was us or another family — no one else could be saved, no matter what creative plans we had, and we did have them. It could only be one family. But then the dream sped up — we would rebuild civilization.

It wouldn't matter.

The evil of man would continue — the violence would return and this massive death would have been in vain. Like Cain, humanity would wander through generations and generations merely remorseful, only ever able to swear to do better. Never to do so. All in vain.

I awoke covered in sweat and panting like I'd just come up for air. Noah had already left for the day and I was all alone in our home — we would only have it a few more weeks. I grabbed my pillow and curled my body around it like I did as a young girl and I prayed.

If we are going to do this, O God, may it work. May we truly be reborn and emerge, ready to learn to do good. May we be capable of this great change. May we be willing enough.

MODERN MIDRASH: THE DAY MIRIAM DIED

Was there really no public mourning for Miriam after she died? Or, did it just not make it into the story? When Miriam the Prophet finally dies in the Book of Numbers, all we get is this:

The Israelites — the entire congregation — arrived at the wilderness of Zin on the new moon of the first month, and the people encamped at Kadesh. Miriam died there and was buried there. And there was no water for the congregation, and they joined against Moses and Aaron.[124]

This is *Miriam* we are talking about. The one who is responsible for Moses' conception and rescue on the Nile. Miriam. The one who led us in celebration through the Sea of Reeds to freedom after centuries of servitude. Our water-bearing mother. She was a sustainer, and when she died, as the legend goes, the well that followed her disappeared.

The well was given to the Jewish people in the merit of Miriam; the Pillar of Cloud was in the merit of Aaron; and the manna in the merit of Moses. When Miriam died the well disappeared, as it is stated: "And Miriam died there" (Numbers 20:1), and it says thereafter in the next verse: "And there was no water for the congregation" (Numbers 20:2). But the well returned in the merit of both Moses and Aaron.[125]

At least we learn that Miriam had the honor of dying by *divine kiss* and not the Angel of Death. This puts her in the company of our patriarchs and her brothers.

The Sages taught: There were six people over whom the Angel of Death had no sway in their demise, and they are: Abraham, Isaac, and Jacob, Moses, Aaron, and Miriam… Abraham, Isaac, and Jacob, as it is written with regard to them, respectively: "With everything," "from everything," "everything;" since they were blessed with everything they were certainly spared the anguish of… the Angel of Death… Moses, Aaron, and Miriam, as it is written with regard to them that they died "by the mouth of God," which indicates that they died with a kiss, and not at the hand of the Angel of Death.[126]

But what happened that day? Was she alone, off on a walk, and suddenly stricken down? Was she at home in bed? Did it hurt? What is this story not telling me? What follows is an original modern midrash, written by me, from Miriam's perspective, attempting an answer.

✴✴✴

It was a dawn like any other. The sun was about to peek through the dark sky, the animals were rustling, and the babies were crying and cooing. The only thing different about that day was that it would be my last.

The night before, the Angel Lailah appeared to me in a dream. "Do you recognize me?" she asked. I did, but in a deja vu sort of way. I knew why she was there, though — why she had finally shown her face to me, so long after I first met her. I think I'd known for a while. Call it intuition. My time was coming to a close. "You will be leaving here in the morning," Lailah said. "Right when the sun is fully visible over the horizon, The Source of Life that gave you this go-around on Earth will relieve you of it with a kiss."

I wasn't scared. In fact, I was perfectly at ease. As an elderly woman, walking 'round and 'round this desert only gets harder and harder. I get slower and the new ones — the kids who will inherit our dream — are getting faster.

I'll confess, I had been praying for this mercy to arrive soon. As the sun started rising I contemplated if I should call my loved ones to me. Did I want to be surrounded in my final moments? But as soon as I asked I knew the answer: I already was — my mother's face flashed in my memory, then those left in Egypt. The breeze was warm. The smell was faintly of fire in the distance. Campfire and dust.

Judging by the sky, I had no more than ten minutes and I figured I'd spend those last breaths in song. So I did. I hummed and sang with my eyes open, gazing up until the sky turned bright and I felt the slightest cool tingle on my lips.

After I died, they found me lying on my mat with my palms facing up and my eyes closed. They wept and sang. The people circled my body like ripples. In time, every single Israelite was there. Their tears painted the rocky ground. And though heat left my body quickly, my spirit lingered a moment to share in the moment.

Moses asked for volunteers to bury me outside the campsite, and ten

young women volunteered: descendants of Dinah. They took me tenderly in their arms and sang as they walked me to my final resting spot. Songs I knew. Songs I didn't.

After I was returned to the dust, they each took out their canteens and dripped a drop on my grave. Like they were watering my story. As if to say, in time, this too will blossom. I always did believe in miracles.

MODERN MIDRASH: HULDAH THE INBETWEEN

Have you heard of Huldah? I hadn't either. There isn't a ton of text about her (almost all of it is compiled below). But the less text there is, the more I want to know. A descendant of Rachav and Joshua, she was a prophet — *the* prophet to advise King Josiah after the Book of Deuteronomy was brought to him — the scroll found in the Temple walls. She was a teacher, and the evidence that indicates that she was fairly unimpressed with authority makes me think we would have been fast and close friends. So please, enjoy learning about this dramatically unsung leader. Huldah, this one's for you.

In the TaNaKh we hear about Huldah in the Book of 2 Kings. The text is as follows:

Hilkiah the high priest said to Shaphan the secretary, "I have found the Book of the Law in the Temple of God." He gave it to Shaphan, who read it. Then Shaphan the secretary went to the king and reported to him: "Your officials have paid out the money that was in the Temple of God and have entrusted it to the workers and supervisors at the Temple." Then Shaphan the secretary informed the king, "Hilkiah the priest has given me a book." And Shaphan read from it in the presence of the king.

When the king heard the words of the Book of the Law, he tore his robes.

He gave these orders to Hilkiah the priest, Ahikam son of Shaphan, Akbor son of Micaiah, Shaphan the secretary and Asaiah the king's attendant: "Go and inquire of God for me and for the people and for all Judah about what is written in this book that has been found. Great is God's anger that burns against us because those who have gone before us have not obeyed the words of this book; they have not acted in accordance with all that is written there concerning us."

Hilkiah the priest, Ahikam, Akbor, Shaphan and Asaiah went to speak to the prophet Huldah, who was the wife of Shallum son of Tikvah, the son of Harhas, keeper of the wardrobe. She lived in Jerusalem, in the New Quarter. She said to them, "This is what God, the God of Israel, says: Tell the man who sent you to me, 'This is what God says: I am going to bring disaster on this place and its people, according to everything written in the book the king of Judah has read. Because they have forsaken me and burned incense to other gods and aroused my anger by all the idols their hands have made, my anger will burn against this place and will not be quenched.' Tell the king of Judah, who sent you to inquire of God, 'This is what God, the God of Israel, says concerning the words you heard: Because your heart was responsive and you humbled yourself before God when you heard what I have spoken against this place and its people — that they would become a curse and be laid waste — and because you tore your robes and wept in my presence, I also have heard you, declares God. Therefore I will gather you to your ancestors, and you will be buried in peace. Your eyes will not see all the disaster I am going to bring on this place.'" So they took her answer back to the king.[127]

We read a very similar narrative in 2 Chronicles 34. And then the Rabbis wonder, why was she sought out if she was alive during the time of Jeremiah, one of the greatest prophets that ever lived in Judea?

Huldah was a prophetess, as it is written: "So Hilkiah the priest and Ahikam and Achbor and Shaphan and Asaiah went to Huldah the prophetess" (II Kings 22:14) as emissaries of King Josiah. The Gemara asks: But if Jeremiah was found there, how could she prophesy? Out of respect for Jeremiah, who was her superior, it would have been fitting that she not prophesy in his presence. The Sages of the school of Rav say in the name of Rav: Huldah was a close relative of Jeremiah, and he did not object to her prophesying in his presence. The Gemara asks: But how could Josiah himself ignore Jeremiah and send emissaries to Huldah? The Sages of the school of Rabbi Shayla say: It is because women are more compassionate, and he hoped that what she would tell them would not be overly harsh.[128]

It was her compassion, the Sages of the school of Rabbi Sheila assume, that won her this prophecy gig. Yet, in the text to follow, Rav Nahman claims she is haughty.

An additional point is mentioned with regard to the prophetesses. Rav Nahman said: Haughtiness is not befitting a woman. And a proof of this is that there were two haughty women, whose names were identical to the names of loathsome creatures. One, Deborah, was called a hornet, as her Hebrew name, Devorah, means hornet; and one, Huldah, was called a marten [similar to a weasel], as her name is the Hebrew term for that creature. From where is it known that they were haughty? With regard to Deborah, the hornet, it is written: "And she sent and called Barak" (Judges 4:6), but she herself did not go to him. And with regard to Huldah, the marten, it is written: "Say to the man that sent you to me" (II Kings 22:15), but she did not say: Say to the king.[129]

So which is it? Compassionate or haughty? Both maybe? Or do these texts show that not much is known of Huldah at all? First she is judged on her sex. Then she is judged by her name. Writer and teacher Rabbi Neal Gold provides us with a few more interesting details about Huldah's life. In an essay on this little-known prophetess he writes:

Most remarkably, the rabbis saw her as an important teacher of Torah in her day. According to Targum Yonatan, an early translation of the

Prophets into Aramaic, she regularly taught at the ulpana, or Hebrew school, of her neighborhood. Furthermore, a set of gates in the southern wall of Jerusalem leading to the Temple Mount were known as the "Huldah Gates," which, although sealed shut for centuries, can still be seen on a tour of Jerusalem today. We may imagine that these were the gates at which Huldah herself once sat, teaching Torah to her disciples.[130]

While we have a few glimpses into who this prophet was, they surround only one event in her life. Is that enough to be life-defining? Who really was Huldah? What is this story not telling me? What follows is an original modern midrash, written by me, from Huldah's perspective, attempting an answer.

✳✳✳

It was my ima who taught me to read but my aba who named me. His grandmother used to tell stories about the magical power of weasels — how they lived lives in the in-between spaces. They would come and go from the spiritual and physical worlds and bring messages. Some thought they were good omens. Some thought they were wicked. Probably a little of both, I imagine — is anything only one way? And they were fiercely protective of their families. So, as soon as I was born — twilight on Rosh Chodesh Elul — Huldah I would be called and Huldah I would be. Hooly for short.

But like I said, it was my mother who taught me to read. As early as I can remember she was showing me letters — prompting me to repeat their sounds. The letter chet from my name lived deep in my throat. Ema came from a tradition of scribes and was determined to prepare me for her legacy. Our legacy.

Everything changed when I turned seven years old. It started small. I'd wake up in the morning, do my chores, help make breakfast for my sisters, and then I'd hear it. No one else did. It was sort of like the rustling *of pages and it sounded like it was coming from outside our kitchen window. I figured it was the wind or a neighbor. But as the weeks went on it got louder and louder until finally, I couldn't ignore it. So I followed it.*

Shoes tied, I headed out into the limestone city, following this sound. Following, following, following until I came all the way to the Temple. It was a market day and people and animals were swarming about like the chaos before creation. But the sound was louder and louder still. It had now morphed into a symphony of rapids on a river.

I followed the sound right up until the gate and then it stopped. My nose and toes were touching the stone. I put my hands on the Temple to feel the heartbeat and felt it all the way down in my stomach. Suddenly, words were flashing through my mind so fast I could barely keep up. The universe was filling me with its secrets as if it had been holding them in for years and only now had a chance to release them — like falling into bed after a long day.

It took years before I could make sense of what I was receiving. It was all static before I learned to tune in. To be honest, I never fully understood it. All I know is people started treating me differently. Averting their eyes. No longer asking to play. Calling me things. I never understood it — I was never one to be too impressed with others. Weren't we all passing through this lifetime fairly quickly anyway? If there was anything to revere it was the way that, generation after generation, words remained.

Not me. Nothing was that special about me.

MODERN MIDRASH: JEHOSHEBEATH AND THE BOY KING

There are a few stories of women saving baby boys in Torah. A lesser-known one comes in 2 Kings (or 2 Chronicles as quoted below) when Jehoshebeath saves and stows away her nephew and heir to the throne, Joash. Here is how the story goes:

So it came to pass that when Jehu was executing judgment upon the house of Ahab, he came upon the officers of Judah and Azaiah's relatives, who had been attending Azaiah, and slew them. He then searched for Azaiah who was caught hiding in Samaria. Then they brought him to Jehu, put him to death and buried him, for they said, "He is the son of Jehoshaphat, who sought Adonai with all his heart." Then there was no one in the house of Azaiah to hold power over the kingdom.

Now when Athaliah, Azaiah's mother, saw that her son had died, she arose and destroyed all the royal offspring of the house of Judah. But Jehoshebeath, the king's daughter, took Joash the son of Azaiah and stole him away from among the king's sons who were being slain, and put him and his nurse in the bedroom. Because Jehoshebeath, daughter of King Jehoram and wife of Jehoiada the kohen, was the sister of Azaiah, she could hide him from Athaliah so she could not kill him. He remained hidden with them in the House of God for six years while Athaliah reigned over the land.[131]

A very similar text can be found earlier in 2 Kings 11. What was Jehoshe-beath thinking when she saved baby Joash? What does it mean to save a life? What is this story not telling me? What follows is an original modern midrash, written by me, from Jehoshebeath's perspective, attempting an answer.

✷✷✷

The story of Yocheved's strength was told often in our home. Pregnant with Moses, she'd walk down the street to such harassment it doesn't bear repeating — but her spirit was firm. And when he was born she called a family meeting. "Listen," she said, "this new soul is ours to protect. Who knows what the years will bring, but today we do know we are able to save him. Even if just for the night." And they did. We know how the story goes. For three months he was kept until, again, another family meeting was called. What do we do now? I always wish I knew what was said at that family meeting.

It was this story that was playing in my head when the queen started her madness. How could she kill like that? Destroy her entire family, for what? Some say she truly went mad. Some say it was her way of ending this monarchy which was doomed from the start — taking it into her own hands — some twisted and premature hand of fate.

Ahaziah and I had always been close. As kids, we were inseparable — refusing to eat meals without the other at the table. We'd play hide-and-seek. Every memory feels silly now in comparison to how much I miss him. It's hard to eat. The night Athaliah started her slaughter, I knew I owed it to him to do everything I could.

We went in the middle of the night. Joash, the young prince, was sleeping quietly. Breathing easily and blissfully unaware of the carnage around

him. His nurse gathered the essentials and the rest we would figure out once we arrived at the Temple, where he would remain. That night, the Temple became a fortress.

If I had known it would be six years hiding here with the most dire of consequences for being found, maybe we would have fled. I would have found a life for us somewhere where he could run free, outside. Maybe on the coast so he could dip his toes in the sea. Or maybe we would have boarded a ship and changed our names. I finally understand why Yocheved put Moses in the basket — what it meant for her to "choose life."

Baruch HaShem it has ended. And I know he will become a great king in time. But now he is seven years old and I'm taking him to the forest at midnight. No guards and he must leave his crown at home.

WHAT DOES 'JUDAISM' SAY ABOUT THIS?

Talmudic Judaism is anti-fundamentalist. It isn't simply the answer that is prized, it is the argument itself, the culture of disputation, the wrestling with the truth. — Rabbi Joseph Telushkin [132]

At the core of Judaism is the devotion to sacred text and to the interpretative process that continually recreates the text. — Rabbi Rachel Adler [133]

Whenever something happens in the world, we wonder, *What does so-and-so have to say about this?* What is the Jewish perspective? What is the progressive perspective? What is this or that group's perspective? Of course, answers to such questions can't help but be massive generalizations. But what does it mean to turn to a tradition that is fundamentally democratic, disparate, and not dogmatic, as the Jewish tradition is? Does it mean that *Judaism, then, is whatever the Jewish community says it is?*[134] Or does it have at least a few fundamental stakes in the ground that can't be swayed no matter how hard the wind blows?

In a short essay entitled *Wide-Angle Judaism,* my teacher and brilliant Torah scholar Rachel Brodie z"l reflected on this question.

When asked what Judaism says about "x" or "y," I responded with, "Which Judaism? The one understood by Chabad in 19th-century

Belarus? The one practiced by Persian Jews in Iran in the 1970s? The one taught by Maimonides? The one imagined by Abraham Joshua Heschel?" There is no "Judaism;" there are Judaisms.[135]

In the wake of the Supreme Court of the United States ruling to overturn Roe v. Wade, I felt an initial urge to study up on what Jewish wisdom or law has to say about abortion. I have studied this issue to some degree in the past and certainly have read many personal essays from my rabbi friends on the topic, so I kind of knew what I'd find. But then I stopped and considered: what the Jewish tradition has to say about abortion is what the Jewish tradition has to say about any topic, in some way. The plain text is not the conclusion, and not only because the Torah *is [also] lovingly, brilliantly, divinely not clear.*[136] The text itself is not the conclusion because it must pass through interpretive, intuitive, and democratic processes.

Let us start with the Oven of Akhnai, a classic Talmudic story about how Jewish law works in the world. When we don't know how to rule on a particular case do we wait for a voice from heaven to tell us, or do we figure it out, on the ground? The answer is the latter, but here is the story:

THE OVEN OF AKHNAI, FROM TALMUD BAVA METZIA 59B

It is taught: they would cut segments and put sand between one segment and another. Rabbi Eliezer renders ovens made of these segments pure and the Sages render them impure. And this is known as the oven of Akhnai. The Gemara asks: What is the relevance of Akhnai, a snake, in this context? Rav Yehuda said that Shmuel said: It is described in that manner because the Rabbis surrounded it with their statements like this snake — which often forms a coil when at rest — and deemed it impure. The Sages taught: On that day, when they discussed this matter, Rabbi Eliezer provided all possible answers in the world to support his opinion, but the Rabbis did not accept his explanations.

After failing to convince the Rabbis logically, Rabbi Eliezer said to them: If the halakha is in accordance with my opinion, this carob tree will prove it. The carob tree was uprooted from its place one hundred cubits, and some say four hundred cubits. The Rabbis said to him: One does not cite halakhic proof from the carob tree. Rabbi Eliezer then said to them: If the halakha is in accordance with my opinion, the stream will prove it. The water in the stream turned backward and began flowing in the opposite direction. They said to him: One does not cite halakhic proof from a stream.

Rabbi Eliezer then said to them: If the halakha is in accordance with my opinion, the walls of the study hall will prove it. The walls of the study hall leaned inward and began to fall. Rabbi Yehoshua scolded the walls and said to them: If Torah scholars are contending with each other in matters of halakha, what is the nature of your involvement in this dispute? The Gemara relates: The walls did not fall because of the deference due Rabbi Yehoshua, but they did not straighten because of the deference due Rabbi Eliezer, and they are still leaning to this day.

Rabbi Eliezer then said to them: If the halakha is in accordance with my opinion, heaven will prove it. A Divine Voice emerged from heaven and said: Why are you differing with Rabbi Eliezer, as the halakha is in accordance with his opinion in every place that he expresses an opinion?

Rabbi Yehoshua stood on his feet and said: It is written: "It is not in heaven" (Deuteronomy 30:12). The Gemara asks: What is the relevance of the phrase "It is not in heaven" in this context? Rabbi Yirmeya says: Since the Torah was already given at Mount Sinai, we do not give consideration to a Divine Voice, as You already wrote at Mount Sinai, in the Torah: "After a majority to incline" (Exodus 23:2). Since the majority of Rabbis disagreed with Rabbi Eliezer's opinion, the halakha is not ruled in accordance with his opinion. The Gemara relates: Rabbi Natan encountered Elijah the prophet and said to him: What did the Holy One, Blessed be God, do at that time, when Rabbi Yehoshua issued his declaration? Elijah said to him: *The Holy One, Blessed be God, smiled and said: My children have triumphed over Me; My children have triumphed over Me.*

Fundamentally, what the Torah has to say about anything is in the hands of the people who are interpreting it. Does that mean we get to rewrite it? In some ways yes, and also no. It is read through our eyes and interpreted for our own lives. Torah is not dogmatic, but democratic.

To go further, Torah was revealed to each member of the Israelite community. Try not to think of this too literally — try thinking about this mythically, mystically, or metaphorically — but there is the idea that we were all standing at Sinai when the Torah was given. Earlier in this book I said our souls were standing at Sinai. That is a nice way to think about it. The point of this tradition is that the ancient Sages didn't have more connection to the capital-T Truth than we do. Sure, they may have been more learned (which is not to be glossed over and will be addressed soon), but in a way the text already and always has lived inside of us, teaching us how to live, how to stand in awe of this thing we call living.

Here is the text I am talking about:

Another explanation: "And God said all of these things, saying" — Rabbi Yitzchak said, What the prophets were to prophesy in the future in each generation, the Israelites already received from Mount Sinai. As Moses said to Israel (Deuteronomy 29:14), "[The covenant was made] with those standing here with us today and with those not here with us today." It does not say [at the end of the verse], "standing with us today," but rather, "with us today;" these are the souls that will be created in the future who, as of now, do not have substance, about whom "standing" is therefore not mentioned. For even though they did not exist at that time, each one received that which was theirs.[137]

And then, finally, our svara. I learned about svara from a yeshiva named for this very concept, SVARA. In their online resources, they write the following:

Svara is a 2,000-year-old Jewish concept invented by the Rabbis of the Talmud, to refer to one's moral intuition informed by Jewish learning. The Rabbis considered svara a legitimate — and sacred — means of figuring out how we should live our lives, in addition to the means they already had — the Torah. But they valued it as so reliable a source of truth that they considered any law that grew out of their svara to have the same status as that of a truth derived directly from Torah, d'oraita ("straight from the Torah"). In fact, according to Jewish law, svara can even supercede Torah when the two conflict. Svara has been central to the evolution of the Jewish tradition and underlies the radical nature of Jewish thinking itself, but has been, until now, something of a secret of talmudic scholars and rabbis. The crucial element in turning one's moral intuition, insight and life experience into svara is learning.[138]

So what does Jewish tradition say about any topic under the sun? Something like this: start with your own deep learning — studying the laws and wisdom of generations past. Then, tap into your sacred moral intuition — what is your being, which was created in the likeness of the Divine, telling you? Finally, bring that to the community, and together, find an appropriate response.

In her groundbreaking work of Jewish feminist scholarship, S*tanding Again at Sinai: Judaism from a Feminist Perspective*, Judith Plaskow comments on the slippery nature of Torah.

The contrary uses to which the Bible has been put suggest that the needs and values of a community of readers are as much a source of norms as the texts themselves… In our individualistic American culture, this source [of authority] is often identified as the individual, who picks and chooses among texts according to "personal preference."[139]

Amen, Professor Plaskow. I fear we use Jewish tradition as proof text when we agree with it and ignore it when we don't. Look no further than Jews who disagree on abortion. If you look carefully, I'm sure you can find texts that support and negate any position, opinion, or question you have — the prophets show us that even following the laws is eventually called into question as just empty religious theater (Amos 5:21–23, Isaiah 1:13–17).

I'd rather abide by an ethic where Torah is not cherry-picked when convenient but understood as a process — a process of learning and deep contemplation and collaborative problem-solving.

Plaskow continues: *Human beings are fundamentally communal; our individuality is a product of community, and our choices are shaped by our being with others. Scripture itself is a product of community.*[140]

Yes, scripture is a product of community, but it is also a *member* of our community. Ancient wisdom sits at our table. It has a significant voice. But as Rabbi Mordecai Kaplan says: *The ancient authorities are entitled to a vote — but not a veto.*[141]

Let us release from our imaginations this mythic pillar we call Judaism and instead embrace a Jewish way of relating to our world. Instead of asking, *What does "Judaism" say about this?* try asking, *How can we take a Jewish approach to this question?* Or even, *How have Jews approached this question in the past and how are they doing it today?*

And then, after you have done all of that, with as much integrity and painstaking study and consideration as you can, just as you think you have the best answer ever, remember that your neighbor may disagree.

Both these and those are the words of the living God.[142]

Let's end with a classic Jewish joke.

Once there was a new rabbi with a very big problem. Every prayer service the people would start arguing about what to do for the Shema. Half of the congregants were sitting and half were standing. The standing ones were yelling, "Stand up! We stand for the Shema!" The sitting ones were yelling, "Sit down! We sit for the Shema!" The rabbi didn't know what to do. Luckily, someone suggested she go and ask the oldest congregant, who was in fact a founding member. They could know once and for all what the tradition was.

So the next day she went to the elder's home and asked: "Is the tradition to stand when we chant the Shema?"

The elder answered, "No, that is not the tradition."

The rabbi said, "Then the tradition must be to sit when we chant the Shema!"

The elder answered, "No, that is also not the tradition."

The rabbi said, "Well then what is it, because all the people seem to be able to do is argue about whether they should sit or stand."

The elder smiled and said, "THAT is the tradition."

PLAYGROUND

In the beginner's mind there are many possibilities; in the expert's mind there are few. — Shunryu Suzuki, *Zen Mind, Beginner's Mind* [143]

Torah study is one continuous game with no scoreboard and no trophies. If someone were to say they have learned all there is to know about Torah, they would be admitting they haven't. There is always more to learn and reconsider and reapply to our ever-changing world.

In fact, the mindset of a student of Torah is similar in many ways to a Zen Buddhist — Beginner's mind.[144] One's mind has to be open and willing to look at the text with fresh ideas and curiosity. No matter how many times this person has met the text before, they must engage with it as if they are a beginner. This is a posture of humility and reverence for the text. The reader must ask, who am I to claim I know everything there is to know?

To approach a text with an open mind is to approach the text with a willingness to play. If your mind is truly open, you have no predetermined agenda for the text and no conclusion you are hoping to find. All you do is explore.

Sometimes I imagine I am shrunk to the size of an ant (like in the late 80's classic, *Honey, I Shrunk the Kids*) and walking through the columns of text like I'm playing hopscotch on a playground. Oh, what does that say? Huh, what's happening over there? Discovering ideas, even ones I've seen before. Sometimes I imagine a text is like a play structure. Some people want to hang out on the monkey bars all day, testing their skills. Others are trying to walk up the slide or use some other part of the structure in new ways. Sometimes we forgo playing what we want to play so we can join in an organized game of lava monster. Such is the compromise of playing in groups.

When I skip around the text this way, I can suspend concepts normally brought into more academic study, like being right or wrong. I'm able to dig into the dirty mess of Torah and make a mud pie. Being in a state of play is a place beyond being right and wrong — a place of pure possibility. It behooves us to pause here and read the ensnaring words of Israeli poet, Yehuda Amichai:

The Place Where We Are Right
By Yehuda Amichai

From the place where we are right
Flowers will never grow
In the spring.

The place where we are right
Is hard and trampled
Like a yard.

But doubts and loves
Dig up the world
Like a mole, a plow.
And a whisper will be heard in the place
Where the ruined
House once stood.

I'm not trying to claim that the content of Torah preaches complete moral relativity or that Jewish tradition doesn't have clear boundaries about things that are egregiously wrong or right. That would be a fool's errand. And it would be inaccurate. I'm saying that approaching a text isn't only about making these moral judgments. Sometimes, a text is a field to explore. We turn now to Rumi, who also once wrote of a field:

Out Beyond Ideas
by Rumi

Out beyond ideas of wrongdoing and rightdoing,
there is a field. I'll meet you there.

When the soul lies down in that grass,
the world is too full to talk about.
Ideas, language, even the phrase each other
doesn't make any sense.

What would we gain from thinking about study as play? How might this idea soften or loosen us? What might we uncover?

THE BELIEF GAME

It is a sign of childishness to accept the great religious myths as literal truths, a sign of adolescence to regard them as delusion, and a sign of maturity to appreciate their spiritual implications.
— Rabbi Mordecai Kaplan [145]

What is important then about the Torah-Book is not that it is all factual but that even where it is not it is still meaningful.
— Rabbi Milton Steinberg [146]

I do not believe there was a revelation at Sinai; I do believe that I was there. — Leonard Fein [147]

The second most common question I get when teaching the Torah to kids is *Did this really happen?* (The most common is: *Can I go to the restroom?*). To this question I always reply, *What do you think?* Depending on what part of the Torah the question is about, I get all sorts of answers from, *No way*, to, *Well, maybe it happened but not exactly like this*, to the ever-imaginationally gifted, *Why not?*

The topics that evoke the most did-it-really-happen questions are miracles and the extremely long lifespans of early biblical figures. Did Methuselah, Noah's grandfather, actually live to be 969 years old? Did that donkey *really* just talk? How did trumpets tooting make the walls of Jericho fall down?

Then I ask something like, How does the story change for you if it did or didn't happen? In other words, reading the Torah as if every single word in it literally happened is only one of many ways for it to be true or real. Just because it didn't really happen in a physical or literal sense doesn't mean you can't believe in it. If anything, the most intellectually honest position is to surrender to agnosticism.

The Torah's entire value and eternal wisdom do not necessarily hinge on it being the exact documentation of ancient history. Of course, for many Jews (and Christians and Muslims alike), much of what is described in the Torah (if not all of it) did actually happen as it says. Yes. End of story. But I can't help but wonder, if that was its only or even primary value, why would we need to interpret it? Wouldn't we try to memorize it, or listen to it in utter silence, bathe in its revelation, and then go home? Of course, this was the cosmic shift that occurred during the time of the Rabbis: the move from prophecy to analysis.

If not the exact accuracy of its narrative, what might we believe in when it comes to the Torah?

We might believe that through the act of study, we draw closer to the Spirit of the Universe — study as a form of prayer. Like the great Medieval Sephardic Jewish philosopher commonly known as Maimonides, we might believe we are unpacking great metaphors of God. We might believe that the layers of exegesis available to the reader mirror the Truth about how life actually works — that our ultimate purpose is to deepen our creative potential and awaken, awaken, awaken. Or we might believe that we don't work on Torah so much as Torah works on us. It hones us like a pencil sharpener so that we are more fit to lead lives of goodness. A sort of meta-parent. We can believe in the Torah without believing the plain sense of its account.

Then there's the question of real and pretend — a binary we take for granted. Many assume today, in the secular world, that there is a truer

Truth that we have access to than our ancient forebears—that we have evolved so far beyond the writers of the Hebrew Bible that they ought not to be taken seriously. We condescend to them. We might call our Truth science or reason. And we might be right. But perhaps we could see wisdom as additive and not monolithic. When we let newer ways of knowing *completely* supersede those of our ancestors, we cut ourselves off from other roads to wisdom. Story and poetry teach in ways math never can (and of course, vice versa).

Here's an example. At the end of Moses' life, at the ripe old age of 120, he climbs to the top of Mt. Nebo and even though *his eyes were undimmed and his vigor unabated*,[148] he dies. He dies looking out upon the land flowing with milk and honey. He dies after 40 years of shepherding the Israelites through the desert (not even having wanted the job). He dies unable to taste the sweetness he has helped provide to the next generation. Of course he dies. This isn't tragic. This is the natural course of things. You can't live to see it all, and eventually, every leader needs to stay behind, even if they aren't ready to. It is our nature to pass the torch—the people need a Joshua to arise. Life spins on.

So did Moses actually die on a mountain at 120 years of age? Probably not. Do I believe in the value and power of this story? Yes, I do.

Now allow me to argue with myself. I wonder if the word belief or the orientation of *believing* in the Torah is not fitting. Indeed, the primary Jewish orientation to the Divine is not one of belief but of partnership or wrestling. (I like to think of wrestling as we think of the sport, which often looks more like dance.) Let us look at the blessing we say before studying Torah. Here is my highly interpretive translation:

Blessed are You, Divine Organization of the Universe, our Oneness, Source of all who makes us holy with mitzvot, commanding us to engage with words of Torah.

Not believe. Not fact-check. Not prove. Engage.

But if we are to entertain the idea that belief is a crucial orientation towards the Torah, let's try a little thought experiment. Consider the belief *Everything happens for a reason*. Personally, this phrase drives me nuts. Yet, it is a belief that we can assume Joseph holds dear. He believes that the will of God works to orchestrate people's lives for certain reasons. This Genesis story goes as follows: Joseph was sold into slavery by his brothers. He eventually ends up in a dungeon in Egypt. The Pharaoh discovers he can interpret dreams, and soon, he becomes not only the acting ruler of Egypt, but his foresight allows him to plan ahead and save the Egyptians and surrounding peoples from famine. After Joseph finally reveals his true identity to his brothers (who come down to Egypt seeking food because the famine has reached them, too) he quickly says the following:

Now, do not be distressed or reproach yourselves because you sold me hither; it was to save life that God sent me ahead of you. It is now two years that there has been famine in the land, and there are still five years to come in which there shall be no yield from tilling. God has sent me ahead of you to ensure your survival on earth, and to save your lives in an extraordinary deliverance. So, it was not you who sent me here, but God.[149]

On the one hand, maybe Joseph is back to his ways of grandiose self-importance (repeat: *to ensure your survival on earth... in an extraordinary deliverance*). On the other hand, what a way to deal with adversity! Good on you, Joe! He was severely bullied by his brothers but never faltered in knowing his own worth. Even in the dungeons, when he had nothing to offer, he offered his mind and unique skills in reading dreams. Now, he has risen in status and come to face his bullies (yes, he has gotten a wee bit of revenge) and shows that he bears no (or at least minimal?) resentment. He has widened his perspective and understands his life's purpose.

It was not you who sent me here, but God.

And not just so he can show them he rose above it, but because something bigger was coming: the famine. For the entire family and region to be saved, Joseph had to have been in Egypt.

I still don't like the phrase *Everything happens for a reason* because I can cite too many examples of what seem to be completely reasonless violence, death, and suffering that don't result in saving an entire region from famine. (Also, I think this phrase implies that everything turned out OK and that of course isn't always the case.) So how do I square Joseph's deep faith with what I feel in my kishkas?

Perhaps we can focus instead on the *result* of Joseph's belief. Joseph's faith allows him to look beyond his brothers' mistreatment of him. It allows him to move forward and not get hung up on sibling rivalry. Perhaps what's important is not so much the belief itself, but what behaviors the belief allows for or encourages. Perhaps we ought to reverse-engineer ourselves—what behaviors do we hope for, and what beliefs will get us there?

For Joseph, his beliefs in his purpose and the will of God allowed him to reunite with his family—to heal, forgive, and rescue an entire region from famine. How can this idea be applied to Torah?

When we read Torah with a healthy balance of shrewd skepticism and willing reverence, we are positioned to be the most open-minded and open-hearted. We are neither too quick to affirm nor too quick to condemn the text. We are curious and humble, able to equally listen and dispute. This, to me, is how I want to engage with my tradition. I want to take the balanced path that is grateful for and indebted to the wisdom I've received but doesn't discount my agency and ability to incorporate new sources of wisdom.

How are your beliefs about Torah shaping how you approach it? What if you tried on a new belief just for the chance to read the text in new ways? What might you discover?

LAST THINGS

AFTERWORD: WRITE IT, DO IT

Values and stories are empty and meaningless if we lack ways to act upon them. — Rabbi Rachel Adler [150]

Even if I am writing this to no one — if not one soul has picked up this book or read it thus far — it has fulfilled half of its purpose. *I* have fulfilled my purpose. At the end of the Book of Deuteronomy, we are told, *Write for yourselves this song,* referring either to the Torah writ large or to the poem that comes in the following chapter. Regardless, we are talking about Torah. We are asked to write out our own Torah. The final commandment, lucky number 613: write it. So, whether you are reading or not, I have done that. But of course, there is a second part to that verse:

Write for yourselves this song and teach it to the Children of Israel. Place it into their mouths, so that this song will be for Me as a witness for the children of Israel.[151]

Bear witness to the Torah for future generations. Write it so you may sustain it. Write it so you may teach and learn and do. It is Rabbi Akiva who reminds us that study does not remain as words on the page but changes our behavior.[152]

Rabbi Tarfon and the Elders were once reclining in the loft of Nithza's house, in Lod, when this question was posed to them: Which is greater, study or action? Rabbi Tarfon answered, saying: Action is greater. Rabbi Akiva answered, saying: Study is greater. All the rest agreed with Akiva that study is greater than action because it leads to action.[153]

I hope this book will seep into your daily life and not stay on the shelf. After all, Torah is not just *about* how to live, it is *lived*. Torah is asking the proverbial new kid to sit with us. Torah is how we show up to old problems with the eyes of a student. Torah is making for yourself a teacher. Torah is protesting injustice. Torah is pausing to celebrate the changing seasons. This and so much more. When asked to explain the entire Torah on one foot, Hillel the Elder famously says, *What is hateful to you, do not do to your neighbor. That is the whole Torah; the rest is commentary. Go and learn it.*[154]

This book is your invitation to keep learning. There is no expiration date and you can bring as many plus-ones as you'd like. I only hope these pages have warmed you up (maybe you've even broken a sweat). As Rabbi Steven Greenberg writes, *Sacred texts can only say what we are ready to hear.*[155] May you be ready. May you take Torah into your hands and make it sing.

***

Finally, I offer a word on making time for Torah.

There will never be this magical window of time that opens up and pauses the rest of the world's activities so that you can study ancient texts in peace with your beloved chevruta by candlelight in a musky cave by the sea. This will not happen. If Torah is something that is calling to you, you must pause whatever else you're doing before you pick up the phone. If Torah is something you want to learn, may you hear the wisdom of Hillel in the back of your mind:

Say not: "when I shall have leisure I shall study;" perhaps you will not have leisure. [156]

Whether it's Torah or a different great love, now is the time. If it calls to you, answer.

BIBLIOGRAPHY

Adar, Rabbi Ruth. "Why is the Mezuzah Slanted?" Coffee Shop Rabbi: Basic Judaism Spoken Here. April 8, 2019. *https://coffeeshoprabbi.com/2019/04/08/why-is-the-mezuzah-slanted/*. Accessed August 12, 2022.

Adler, Rabbi Rachel. *Engendering Judaism* (Beacon Press: Boston, MA: 1998).

Baden, Joel S. Phd. *The Composition of the Pentateuch: Renewing the Documentary Hypothesis* (Yale University Press: New Haven, CT; 2012).

Brodie, Rachel. *https://www.rachelbrodie.net/by-topic.html*.

Brodie, Rachel, "Wide Angle Judaism" in *Sh'ma: A Journal Of Jewish Ideas*. September 2015. Shma.com. *https://www.rachelbrodie.net/published-work*.

Buber, Martin. *I and Thou*, trans. Walter Kaufmann (Simon and Schuster: New York, NY; 1970).

Buber, Martin. *Tales of the Hasidim: Later Masters* (New York: Schocken Books, 1961).

Cohen, Shaye J.D. *From the Maccabees to the Mishnah*. Third Edition. (Westminster John Knox Press; Louisville, KY; 2014).

Collins, John J. Phd. *Introduction to the Hebrew Bible*, Second Edition (Fortress Press, Minneapolis, MN; 2014).

Fein, Leonard. "Remembering Tomorrow." The Forward. April 29, 2005. *https://forward.com/opinion/3378/remembering-tomorrow/*.

Gillman, Rabbi Neil. *Sacred Fragments: Recovering Theology for the Modern Jew* (Jewish Publication Society: Philadelphia, PA: 1990).

Gold, Rabbi Neal. *Huldah the Prophetess*. MyJewishLearning.com. accessed July 7, 2022.

Greenberg, Rabbi Irving. *The Jewish Way: Living the Holidays* (Simon & Schuster: New York, NY; 1988).

Greenberg, Rabbi Steven. *Wrestling With God & Men: Homosexuality in the Jewish Tradition* (the University of Wisconsin Press: Madison, WI; 2004).

Hammer, Rabbi Jill. *Sisters At Sinai: New Tales Of Biblical Women* (Jewish Publication Society; Philadelphia, PA; 2001).

Heschel, Rabbi Abraham Joshua. *The Sabbath* (Farrar, Straus and Giroux: New York, NY; 1951).

Holtz, Barry W. *Back To The Sources: Reading The Classic Jewish Texts*. Edited by Barry W. Holtz (Simon & Schuster; New York, NY; 1984), 178.

Horn, Dara. Phd. *Eternal Life* (W.W. Norton & Company: NY, New York: 2018).

Kaplan, Rabbi Mordecai M. "The Torah's Fundamental Purpose" in *Dynamic Judaism: The Essential Writings of Mordecai M. Kaplan*. Edited by Emanual S. Goldsmith (Schocken Books: New York, NY; 1985).

Kieval, Herman. *The Curious Case of Kol Nidre*. Commentary Magazine. October 1968. Accessed: *https://www.commentary.org/articles/herman-kieval/the-curious-case-of-kol-nidre/*.

Holzer, Elie with Orit Kent, *A Philosophy of Havruta: Understanding And Teaching The Art Of Text Study In Pairs* (Academic Studies Press: Boston, MA; 2014).

Kukla, Rabbi Elliot and Rabbi Reuben Zellman, "To Wear Is Human, to Live — Divine." in *Torah Queeries: Weekly Commentaries on the Hebrew Bible*, edited by Gregg Drinkwater, Joshua Lesser, and David Shneer (NYU Press; New York, NY; 2009).

Kushner, Rabbi Lawrence. *Honey from the Rock: Visions of Jewish Mystical Renewal* (Jewish Lights Publishing: Woodstock, VT: 1992).

Lamott, Anne. *Bird By Bird: Some Instructions on Writing and Life* (Anchor Books; New York, NY; 1994).

Lau-Lavie, Rabbi Amichai. "She Is The Tree Of Life: D'varim 7:5" from *Below the Bible Belt*. September 15, 2022. *https://amichailaulavie.substack.com/p/she-is-the-tree-of-life*.

Lew, Rabbi Alan. *The Is Real And You Are Completely Unprepared: The Days Of Awe As a Journey Of Transformation* (Back Bay Books: New York, NY: 2002).

Lobdell, Terri. *Driven to succeed: How we're depriving teens of a sense of purpose*. Palo Alto Weekly, November 18, 2011. *https://ed.stanford.edu/news/driven-succeed-how-were-depriving-teens-sense-purpose*.

Morinis, Alan. *With Heart In Mind: Mussar Teachings To Transform Your Life* (Trumpeter Books; Boston, MA; 2014).

Morris, Leon A. "Longing to Hear Again" in *Jewish Theology In Our Time: A New Generation Explores the Foundations and Future of Jewish Belief*, ed. Elliot J. Cosgrove, PhD (Jewish Lights Publishing: Woodstock, VT; 2010).

Mullen, Luba. "How Trees Survive and Thrive After A Fire" from *Your National Forests Magazine*, Summer/Fall 2017. National Forest

Foundation. *https://www.nationalforests.org/our-forests/your-national-forests-magazine/how-trees-survive-and-thrive-after-a-fire*. Accessed Sept 9, 2022.

Neusner, Jacob. *Invitation to the Talmud: A Teaching Book* (Wipf and Stock Publishers; Eugene, OR; 1998).

Oz, Amos and Fania Oz-Salzberger. *Jews and Words* (Yale University Press: New Haven, CT; 2012).

Piercey, Marge, *The Art Of Blessing The Day: Poems with a Jewish Theme* (Alfred A. Knopf, Publisher; New York, 2018).

Plaskow, Judith, Phd. *Standing Again At Sinai: Judaism From A Feminist Perspective* (HarperCollins: New York, NY; 1991).

Robinson, George. *Essential Judaism: A Complete Guide to Beliefs, Customs, and Rituals.* Updated Edition. (Atria Paperback; New York, NY; 2016).

Schorsch, Rabbi Ismar. "Behind God's Names." Jewish Theological Seminary Torah Online. November 20, 1993. Accessed July 28, 2022. *https://www.jtsa.edu/Torah/behind-gods-names/*.

Steinberg, Rabbi Milton. *Basic Judaism* (Harcout, Brace & World, Inc. New York, NY: 1947).

Strassfeld, Rabbi Michael. *The Jewish Holidays: A Guide And Commentary* (William Morrow: New York, NY: 1985).

Suzuki, Shunryu. *Zen Mind, Beginner's Mind* (Shambhala: Boston, MA: 2006).

Telushkin, Rabbi Joseph. *Hillel: If Not Now, When?* (Schocken: New York, NY: 2010).

Trepp, Leo. Judaism: *Development and Life.* Third Edition. (Wadsworth Publishing Company; Belmont, CA: 1982).

Weiss, Michael. *The Anti-Semite's Favorite Jewish Prayer: The centuries-long controversy over Yom Kippur's Kol Nidre.* Slate Magazine. October 7, 2008. Accessed: *https://slate.com/human-interest/2008/10/the-centuries-long-controversy-over-yom-kippur-s-kol-nidre.html*.

Oz, Amos and Fania Oz-Salzberger. *Jews and Words* (Yale University Press: New Haven, CT; 2012).

Piercey, Marge, *The Art Of Blessing The Day: Poems with a Jewish Theme* (Alfred A. Knopf, Publisher; New York, 2018).

Plaskow, Judith, Phd. *Standing Again At Sinai: Judaism From A Feminist*

Perspective (HarperCollins: New York, NY; 1991).

Robinson, George. *Essential Judaism: A Complete Guide to Beliefs, Customs, and Rituals*. Updated Edition. (Atria Paperback; New York, NY; 2016).

Schorsch, Rabbi Ismar. "Behind God's Names." Jewish Theological Seminary Torah Online. November 20, 1993. Accessed July 28, 2022. *https://www.jtsa.edu/Torah/behind-gods-names/*.

Steinberg, Rabbi Milton. *Basic Judaism* (Harcout, Brace & World, Inc. New York, NY: 1947).

Strassfeld, Rabbi Michael. *The Jewish Holidays: A Guide And Commentary* (William Morrow: New York, NY: 1985).

Suzuki, Shunryu. *Zen Mind, Beginner's Mind* (Shambhala: Boston, MA: 2006).

Telushkin, Rabbi Joseph. *Hillel: If Not Now, When?* (Schocken: New York, NY: 2010).

Trepp, Leo. *Judaism: Development and Life*. Third Edition. (Wadsworth Publishing Company; Belmont, CA: 1982).

Weiss, Michael. *The Anti-Semite's Favorite Jewish Prayer: The centuries-long controversy over Yom Kippur's Kol Nidre*. Slate Magazine. October 7, 2008. Accessed: *https://slate.com/human-interest/2008/10/the-centuries-long-controversy-over-yom-kippur-s-kol-nidre.html*.

ENDNOTES

1. Pirkei Avot 5:22
2. Pirkei Avot 2:9
3. R' Simcha Bunim of Peshischa, Kol Mevaser
4. Terri Lobdell. Driven to succeed: How we're depriving teens of a sense of purpose. Palo Alto Weekly, November 18, 2011. https://ed.stanford.edu/news/driven-succeed-how-were-depriving-teens-sense-purpose
5. Rabbi Steven Greenberg, *Wrestling With God & Men: Homosexuality in the Jewish Tradition* (the University of Wisconsin Press: Madison, 2004), 23.
6. Pirkei Avot 2:16
7. Rabbi Milton Steinberg. *Basic Judaism* (Harcout, Brace & World, Inc. New York, NY: 1947), 22.
8. "Old Testament" and the word "Scriptures" are Christian names for this text.
9. This section is found on Rachel Brodie's website in a description section about topics on which she can teach. https://www.rachelbrodie.net/by-topic.html
10. Jacob Neusner, *Invitation to the Talmud: A Teaching Book* (Wipf and Stock Publishers; Eugene, OR; 1998), 28.
11. Ibid., 167.
12. Deuteronomy 34:7
13. George Robinson, *Essential Judaism: A Complete Guide to Beliefs, Customs, and Rituals, Updated Edition*. (Atria Paperback; New York, NY; 2016), 271.
14. Ibid., 271.
15. Ibid., 271.
16. Recently, many communities have been using the phrases b-mitzvah, b'mitzvah or bet mitzvah as gender inclusive persons of bar/bat Mitzvah.
17. Martin Buber, *I and Thou*, trans. Walter Kaufmann (New York, NY: Simon and Schuster, 1970), 128.
18. Rabbi Abraham Joshua Heschel. *The Sabbath* (Farrar, Straus and Giroux: New York, NY; 1951), 16.
19. Anne Lamott, *Bird By Bird: Some Instructions on Writing and Life* (Anchor Books; New York, NY; 1994), 77.

20 Ismar Schorsch, "Behind God's Names." *https://www.jtsa.edu/*. November 20, 1993. Accessed July 28, 2022.
21 Rabbi Leon A Morris. "Longing to Hear Again" in *Jewish Theology In Our Time: A New Generation Explores the Foundations and Future of Jewish Belief*, ed. Elliot J. Cosgrove, PhD (Woodstock, VT: Jewish Lights Publishing, 2010), 135.
22 Genesis 28:16–17
23 Ismar Schorsch, "Behind God's Names." *https://www.jtsa.edu/*. November 20, 1993. Accessed July 28, 2022.
24 Jeremiah 2:13, 17:13
25 Genesis 1:1–2
26 Exodus 3:13–15
27 Judith Plaskow. *Standing Again At Sinai: Judaism From A Feminist Perspective* (HarperCollins, New York; 1991), 138-140.
28 Pirkei Avot 3:2
29 Zohar 2:100b
30 Emily Dickinson, *The Complete Poems of Emily Dickinson*. Boston: Little, Brown, 1924; Bartleby.com, 2000. *www.bartleby.com/113/*. Accessed April 20, 2017.
31 Dara Horn, Phd. *Eternal Life* (W.W. Norton & Company: NY, New York: 2018), 74–75.
32 Genesis 3:19
33 Deuteronomy 30:19
34 Marge Piercey, "Meditation before reading Torah," from *The Art Of Blessing The Day: Poems with a Jewish Theme* (Alfred A. Knopf, Publisher; New York, 2018), 134.
35 Genesis 2:9
36 Genesis 3:22
37 Leviticus 19:23–25
38 Avot de Rabbi Nathan, 31b
39 Rabbi Amichai Lau-Lavie, "She Is The Tree Of Life: D'varim 7:5" from *Below the Bible Belt*. September 15, 2022. *https://amichailaulavie.substack.com/p/she-is-the-tree-of-life*
40 Bemidbar Rabbah 13:1
41 Numbers 11:17

42 Shir HaShirim 4:11
43 Ezra ben Solomon on Shir HaShirim 4:11:1
44 Rashi on Shir HaShirim 4:11:2
45 Ezra ben Solomon on Shir HaShirim 4:11:1 Psalm 19:9–11
46 Ezekiel 3:1–4
47 Kohelet 1:26
48 Jerusalem Talmud, Kiddushin 4:12
49 Luba Mullen, "How Trees Survive and Thrive After A Fire" from *Your National Forests Magazine*, Summer/Fall 2017. National Forest Foundation. https://www.nationalforests.org/our-forests/your-national-forests-magazine/how-trees-survive-and-thrive-after-a-fire. Accessed Sept 9, 2022.
50 Jerusalem Talmud, Shekalim 6:1
51 Exodus 3:2–3
52 Leviticus 18:5
53 Ezekiel 20:11
54 Deuteronomy 30:11–14
55 Deuteronomy 31:19
56 Michael Weiss, *The Anti-Semite's Favorite Jewish Prayer: The centuries-long controversy over Yom Kippur's Kol Nidre*. Slate Magazine. October 7, 2008. Accessed: https://slate.com/human-interest/2008/10/the-centuries-long-controversy-over-yom-kippur-s-kol-nidre.html
57 Herman Kieval, *The Curious Case of Kol Nidre*. Commentary Magazine. October 1968. Accessed: https://www.commentary.org/articles/herman-kieval/the-curious-case-of-kol-nidre/
58 Kieval, Ibid.
59 Rabbi Alan Lew. *The Is Real and You Are Completely Unprepared: The Days Of Awe As a Journey Of Transformation* (Back Bay Books: New York, NY: 2002), 37.
60 Joshua 1:1
61 Rabbi Michael Strassfeld, *The Jewish Holidays: A Guide and Commentary* (William Morrow: New York, NY: 1985), 107.
62 Ibid.
63 Martin Buber, *Tales of the Hasidim: Later Masters* (New York: Schocken Books, 1961), 249–250.

64 Kohelet 3:6–7
65 "R. Judah the son of R. Shalum said: 'There is actually no such thing as preceding or following in the Torah.'" Midrash Tanhuma Teruma 8.
66 Rabbi Abraham Joshua Heschel. *The Sabbath* (Farrar, Straus and Giroux: New York; 1951), 97, 99–100.
67 Midrash Tanchuma, Pekudei 3
68 Amos Oz and Fania Oz-Salzberger. *Jews and Words* (Yale University Press, New Haven; 2012), 121–122.
69 Numbers 11:7
70 Amos Oz and Fania Oz-Salzberger. *Jews and Words* (Yale University Press, New Haven; 2012), 126.
71 Rabbi Steven Greenberg, *Wrestling With God & Men: Homosexuality in the Jewish Tradition* (the University of Wisconsin Press: Madison, 2004), 32.
72 Genesis 4:9
73 Talmud Ta'anot 7a
74 Ibid.
75 Elie Holzer with Orit Kent, *A Philosophy of Havruta: Understanding and Teaching the Art of Text Study in Pairs* (Academic Studies Press: Boston, MA; 2014), 60–61.
76 Ibid., 75.
77 I've heard this ethos of chevruta most beautifully articulated by Rabbi Benay Lappe while attending SVARA's Queer Talmud Camp in 2019 at Walker Creek Ranch, California.
78 Pirkei Avot 4:1
79 Deuteronomy 6:6–7
80 Alan Morinis, *With Heart In Mind: Mussar Teachings To Transform Your Life* (Trumpeter Books; Boston, MA; 2014), 20.
81 Pirkei Avot 4:12
82 Mishnah Berakhot 1:3
83 Talmud, Berakhot 28a
84 Rabbi Rachel Adler. *Engendering Judaism* (Beacon Press: Boston, MA: 1998), 1.
85 Leo Trepp, *Judaism: Development and Life*. Third Edition. (Wadsworth Publishing Company; Belmont, CA: 1982), 188.

86 Genesis 11:1–9
87 Of course, translation matters, and yes, there is even some dispute about the Hebrew if you go really down this rabbit hole
88 Talmud Sanhedrin 17a
89 Deuteronomy 21:18–21
90 Talmud Sanhedrin 71a
91 Rabbi Elliot Kukla and Rabbi Reuben Zellman, "To Wear Is Human, to Live — Divine." in *Torah Queeries: Weekly Commentaries on the Hebrew Bible*, by Gregg Drinkwater (Editor), Joshua Lesser (Editor), David Shneer (Editor) (NYU Press, 2009), 255.
92 The following section is in reference to Mishnah Sheviit 10
93 Deuteronomy 15:9
94 Mishnah Gittin 4:3
95 Rabbi Joseph Telushkin. *Hillel: If Not Now, When?* (Schocken: New York, NY: 2010), 56–57.
96 Rabbi Mordecai M. Kaplan, "The Torah's Fundamental Purpose" in *Dynamic Judaism: The Essential Writings of Mordecai M. Kaplan*. Edited by Emanual S. Goldsmith (Schocken Books: New York, NY; 1985) 89≈90.
97 Talmud Menachot 99a–b
98 Ezra 7:6
99 John J. Collins, *Introduction to the Hebrew Bible*, Second Edition (Fortress Press, Minneapolis, MN; 2014), 456.
100 Ibid., 455.
101 Shaye J.D. Cohen, *From the Maccabees to the Mishnah*. Third Edition. (Westminster John Knox Press; Louisville, KY; 2014), 182.
102 Ezra 7:10: For Ezra had dedicated himself to study the Teaching of God so as to observe it, and to teach laws and rules to Israel
103 Nehemiah 8:1–13
104 Shaye J.D. Cohen, *From the Maccabees to the Mishnah*. Third Edition. (Westminster John Knox Press; Louisville, KY; 2014), 137.
105 Judith Plaskow. *Standing Again at Sinai: Judaism from a Feminist Perspective* (HarperCollins, New York; 1991), 17.
106 Much of the information on Documentary Hypothesis comes from

the following texts: Joel S. Baden. *The Composition of the Pentateuch: Renewing the Documentary Hypothesis* (Yale University Press, New Haven; 2012) and John J. Collins. *Introduction to the Hebrew Bible*, Second Edition (Fortress Press, Minneapolis: 2014)

107 Baden. *The Composition of the Pentateuch: Renewing the Documentary Hypothesis* (Yale University Press, New Haven; 2012), 14.
108 Leviticus 18:22
109 Leviticus 20:13
110 Exodus 22:20 and 23:9
111 Leviticus 19:34 and Leviticus 20:1
112 Leviticus 19:18
113 Deuteronomy 10:19 and 23:8
114 Talmud Shevu'ot 20b
115 Rabbi Irving Greenberg. "Rebirth and Renewal: High Holy Days." Essay. *The Jewish Way: Living the Holidays* (Simon & Schuster: New York: 1988.)196–97.
116 Rabbi Ruth Adar, "Why is the Mezuzah Slanted?" Coffee Shop Rabbi: Basic Judaism Spoken Here. April 8, 2019. *https://coffeeshoprabbi.com/2019/04/08/why-is-the-mezuzah-slanted/*. Accessed August 12, 2022.
117 Barry W. Holtz, *Back to the Sources: Reading The Classic Jewish Texts*. Edited by Barry W. Holtz (Simon & Schuster; New York, NY; 1984), 185.
118 Ibid., 178.
119 *Bereishit Rabbah* 38:13
120 Barry W. Holtz, *Back to the Sources: Reading The Classic Jewish Texts*. Edited by Barry W. Holtz (Simon & Schuster; New York, NY; 1984),180.
121 Genesis 3:1–7
122 *Bereishit Rabbah* 23:3
123 Ramban on Genesis 4:22:1
124 Numbers 20:1–2
125 Talmud Taanit 9a:9
126 Talmud Bava Batra 17a, same "divine kiss" attested in Talmud Mo'ed Katan 28a
127 2 Kings 22:8–20
128 Talmud Megillah 14b

129 Ibid.
130 Rabbi Neal Gold. Huldah the Prophetess. *MyJewishLearning.com*. Accessed July 7, 2022.
131 2 Chronicles 22:8–12
132 Rabbi Joseph Telushkin, Hillel: *If Not Now, When?* (Schocken: New York, NY: 2010), 84.
133 Rabbi Joseph Telushkin, Hillel: *If Not Now, When?* (Schocken: New York, NY: 2010), 84.
134 Rabbi Neil Gillman, *Sacred Fragments: Recovering Theology for the Modern Jew* (Jewish Publication Society: Philadelphia, PA: 1990), 21.
135 Rachel Brodie, "Wide Angle Judaism" in *Sh'ma: A Journal Of Jewish Ideas*. September 2015. *shma.com*
136 Rabbi Steven Greenberg, *Wrestling With God & Men: Homosexuality in the Jewish Tradition* (University of Wisconsin Press: Madison, 2004), 210.
137 Shemot Rabbah 28
138 *svara.org*
139 Judith Plaskow. *Standing Again at Sinai: Judaism from a Feminist Perspective* (HarperCollins, New York; 1991), 19.
140 Ibid.
141 Rabbi Mordecai M. Kaplan, "Observations" in *Dynamic Judaism: The Essential Writings of Mordecai M. Kaplan*. Edited by Emanual S. Goldsmith (Schocken Books: New York, NY; 1985) 105.
142 Talmud Eruvin 13b
143 Shunryu Suzuki, Zen Mind, Beginner's Mind (Shambhala; Boston, MA: 2006), 2.
144 The concept of Beginner's Mind is beautifully explained in Shunryu Suzuki's *Zen Mind, Beginner's Mind* (Shambhala; Boston, MA: 2006).
145 Rabbi Mordecai M. Kaplan, "Observations" in *Dynamic Judaism: The Essential Writings of Mordecai M. Kaplan*. Edited by Emanual S. Goldsmith (Schocken Books: New York, NY; 1985) 104.
146 Rabbi Milton Steinberg. *Basic Judaism* (Harcout, Brace & World, Inc. New York, NY: 1947), 28.
147 Leonard Fein, "Remembering Tomorrow." The Forward. https://

forward.com/opinion/3378/remembering-tomorrow/. April 29, 2005.
148 Deuteronomy 34:7
149 Genesis 45:5–8
150 Rabbi Rachel Adler. *Engendering Judaism* (Beacon Press: Boston, MA: 1998), 25.
151 Deuteronomy 31:19
152 Talmud Kiddushin 40b
153 Ibid.
154 Talmud Shabbat 31a
155 Rabbi Steven Greenberg, *Wrestling With God & Men: Homosexuality in the Jewish Tradition* (the University of Wisconsin Press: Madison, 2004), 221.
156 Pirkei Avot 2:4

www.ingramcontent.com/pod-product-compliance
Lightning Source LLC
Chambersburg PA
CBHW051946290426
44110CB00015B/2135